You Owe Me

You Owe Me

The Emotional Debts
That Cripple Relationships

By
Eric J. Cohen, Ph.D.
and Gregory Sterling

Requests for permission should be addressed to:
New Horizon Press
P.O. Box 669
Far Hills, NJ 07931

Cohen, Eric J. and Sterling, Gregory
    You Owe Me: The Emotional Debts That Cripple Relationships

Interior Design: Susan Sanderson

Library of Congress Catalog Card Number: 98-68325

ISBN: 0-88282-178-4

New Horizon Press
Manufactured in the U.S.A.

2003 2002 2001 2000 1999 / 5 4 3 2 1

AUTHORS' NOTE

The concepts and theories of this book were developed by both authors over countless hours of in-depth discussions about the mysterious nature of relationships. Their close collaboration encompassed all facets of the project—from idea development to writing the text. Dr. Cohen's research and experience counseling couples, as well as his clients' real-life experiences, have served to substantiate the authors' intriguing new approach to understanding relationships. Fictitious identities and names have been given to all characters in this book in order to protect individual privacy.

TABLE OF CONTENTS

INTRODUCTION

Something kept nagging at me. Over eighteen years of clinical practice I had worked with hundreds of couples through the challenges, stresses and heartbreaks of their relationships. But so often my clients and I were vexed by the difficulty of understanding the idiosyncrasies of their unique relationship dynamics and by the struggle to achieve a common language through which they could accurately express their deepest wants and needs. Why were couples so often locked in a drawn-out battle of misunderstanding and exasperation, as if speaking to one another in a foreign tongue?

What I couldn't let go of was the notion that there had to be a more fundamental approach to relationship issues, some basic, common vocabulary that I could use with clients which would provide a readily accessible pathway direct to the heart of their problems. Such a simplifying, shared language could serve to clarify core issues in an unmistakable, non-threatening way, facilitating better communication and more effective problem solving.

In getting to the core of my clients' problems, I considered why I kept hearing the same kinds of despairing exclamations over and over:

- *"It's just not fair after everything I've done for him."*

- *"She's let me down and hurt me so many times and I've just taken it."*

- *"Nothing will ever make up for what he's done to me."*

- *"Where would she be now if it weren't for me?"*

- *"It's always been whatever he wants, whatever will make him happy."*

- *"She never lets me forget."*

- *"He never acknowledges the sacrifices I have made."*

- *"Isn't there some way to settle things between us once and for all?"*

Listening to these heartfelt expressions repeated so often, I realized that imbedded in their meaning was an unmistakable thread of continuity—a theme that echoed forth from disillusioned couples and that kept ringing a familiar note in the back of my brain. Beneath the pain, indignation, sense of betrayal and confusion that plagued partners was a common, pervasive feeling that one person *owed* something to the other. This sense of owing could only be explained by the existence of some form of debt—not financial, but relational. Suddenly it became apparent that the relationships of those I was counseling were all being controlled and poisoned by deep ***emotional debts*** that had never been identified, acknowledged or repaid.

Once the concept of emotional debt took hold, a pragmatic model began to formulate and grow. The ideas evolved spontaneously into an approach that cut to the core and sharply illuminated the realities of relationship conflict between two people. A powerful transformation started to unfold as my clients and I began to see old patterns from an entirely unique and enlightening perspective.

In this new light, as partners unveiled their feelings and described the circumstances which accounted for their guilt, resentment, bitterness and hostility, the underlying forces which governed the relationship could be more easily comprehended and sorted out as the concepts and vocabulary of emotional debt were introduced. Partners could begin to express themselves more accurately and directly in words that were immediately understandable: ***owing, being owed, debtors, creditors, settlements, terms of repayment and debt forgiveness.***

The simplicity and accessibility of the debt model are an outgrowth of what is already a familiar mode of expression to all of us. We live in a world inundated daily by the concepts and language of debt. In our credit card, buy-now-pay-later society, each of us is subtly urged to incur debt all the time. Automobile advertisements and department store salespeople trumpet the idea of "no money down and easy installments" as though the merchandise they want you to trundle off with involves no real cost. Banks and mortgage brokers tout the ease of re-financing or obtaining a line of credit to put that vacation or recreational vehicle or educational degree right within our immediate grasp. The message is that we can have whatever we want when we want—all with a thin piece of plastic or a simple signature on the dotted line to magically defer the reality of payment to some painless future point in time.

We are further anesthetized from the actual cost and responsibility of going into debt by the incessant encouragement we receive to extend ourselves beyond our means. By using the right charge card, we get bonus points, earn cash rebates and accumulate gallons of gas and airline miles. By signing up with the right finance company we can receive anything from Ginsu knives to a Caribbean Island trip. The more you spend the more you get. It is almost elevated to a moral plane—how many pieces of junk mail do we receive that blare out the self-congratulatory exclamation, "You Have Already Been Approved" as though we are being commended for some praiseworthy achievement made possible by our superior character. The message is clear and pervasive: debt is good; debt works; debt is the natural state of man and woman; debt is our gold card to fulfillment.

On a global level, barely a day passes when we do not hear news items about nations in debt, trade deficits or gyrations of international currency exchanges. Countries themselves are referred to as "creditor nations" (Japan and Germany) and "debtor nations" (Russia and Mexico). And until recently, the United States was the greatest of debtor nations, borrowing its way into the delusion of perpetual prosperity. Let the good times roll and pay it all off later (generations later) is the implicit message.

We are both a world *in* debt and a world *of* debtors. We have been conditioned to accept debt as the normal state of affairs—as business as usual. It is the very commonness of debt, the lack of alarm over even trillions of dollars owed, that makes the idea of debt so palatable. We are all seduced into carrying a multitude of debts while the enormity of the burden rarely pierces the forefront of consciousness.

The concept of debt has so infiltrated everyday life that its peculiar terminology has washed through our normal discourse. In truth, it is not so strange to suggest a metaphor for discussing love relationships that utilizes a crossover to the terminology of finance. There already exists a surprising myriad of parallels between the language of love and the seemingly cold nomenclature of the financial world.

For instance, the formal name of most banks includes the appendage "National Trust and Savings Association." Isn't it interesting that *Trust*—one of the most sacred components of love relationships—is also affixed to the name of the most visible symbols of our commercial world? Similarly, many insurance companies use the word *Fidelity* in their name, again lending a hallowed concept of love to the business universe.

There are endless examples of the convergence of relationship terminology and the metaphors of finance. When a debt has been paid off, it is said to have been *satisfied* (perhaps the most sought after goal of relationships). We *make love* and *make money*. We seek emotional *richness* in relationships and avoid *foolish investments* of our time in dead-end *affairs*. We strive to fill both our investment portfolios and emotional relationships with growing *securities*. We continually evaluate the *risks* of *committing* either our dollars or our devotion. We *pledge* both collateral and undying love. Unscrupulous lovers or cheating brokers are seen as *frauds*. Debts that come due are said to be *mature*. None of us would give up our most prized possessions for *love nor money* (with the implication that they are somehow equivalent). Even *losing your shirt* can happen in the bedroom or the boardroom!

There can be no doubt that we already express ourselves through similar language in the very different spheres of relationships and finance. Therefore, I believe the language of debt serves as an accessible and powerful metaphor for delving deep into and reconstructing the intricate dynamics of flesh-and-blood relationships.

At the outset, some individuals may find the common vernacular of business exchange a bit abrasive, sounding as though the complex wonder of human intimacy might be brought down to a sterile level of monetary transaction. However, this new approach has proved itself to be neither reductionistic nor an oversimplification. Instead, the model consistently serves to elevate relationships, not diminish them. By applying a new angle of inquiry into the hidden forces which influence relationships, the inherent elegance and depth of human connection actually emerge more fully. Through the metaphor of financial debt (a concept which everyone in our culture experiences and comprehends all too well), the emotional interweaving and intricacies of human connection in our intimate relationships can be seen in the radiance of a fresh new light.

The uniqueness and power of the debt model is that it incorporates the practical necessity of some give-and-take while allowing kind-hearted acceptance and willing compromise to flourish. As relationship dynamics are aligned through the prism of resolving emotional debt, a sense of internal balance and fairness crystallizes. In this environment, a free exchange can occur naturally, without any impulse for exact accounting or reciprocation.

All human beings share similar relational wants and needs. Each of us seeks security, acceptance, connection, spontaneity and freedom. Our desires might be expressed through different words, but all men and women search for transcendent bonds which provide genuine feelings of satisfaction, excitement and gratitude with the one we love.

When relationships are plagued by emotional debt, creditors are unable to collect, debtors continue to owe and the substance of the emotional debt remains submerged and unacknowledged. Resentment and guilt predominate, minor irritations erupt and a prickly feeling of discomfort pervades the air. The smallest exchange or favor becomes charged with intense emotional energy. Recriminations and victimizations are rampant, and battles over control and submission block the possibility for real intimacy and understanding.

There is so much interfering static and background noise in most relationships—routine stresses, personal aggravations, daily distractions, needling resentments, nit-picking—all of which drown out the intimate connections and potential vibrancy between partners. However, when the cacophony is filtered away and the mundane irritations are dissolved, it becomes unmistakably clear that all couples share certain universal needs and that there are indeed quintessential themes which guide the course of their communications and interactions. As my clients have labored to come to grips with their primary issues and give voice to their frustrations, I have come to realize that the theme of emotional debt has been ringing out over and over again. The theme and the language of debt can provide insight and practical help to all of us who seek vitality and transcendence in our relationships.

Chapter 1

SHATTERED PROMISES, BROKEN HEARTS
The Disillusionment Which Breeds Emotional Debt

If love is blind, marriage is an institution for the blind.
- Anonymous

The average steel-belted radial tire lasts approximately 45,000 miles, or 3.5 years of normal highway use. The duration of the average American marriage is about 2.3 years—which translates into around 30,000 miles of friction and wear. Either way you look at it, we apparently have a more enduring, and often more endearing, relationship with our Michelins and Pirellis than we do with our chosen life partners.

How can this possibly be? How is it that the intense love, binding devotion and earnest commitment of partners standing before the altar can deteriorate faster than the quarter-inch tread of a sixty-nine dollar tire? A lack of sincerity is certainly not the answer. The fact is that virtually every person uttering the vow "till death do us part" truly believes theirs will be a relationship that lasts a lifetime. They may be aware of the dismal statistics of divorce and separation that taint our culture, but somehow, in their hearts, each person feels that "we will be different"—their relationship will prove unique, their tolerance and forbearance sufficient, their love and devotion everlasting.

What is it that actually goes wrong? What causes sincere, well-intentioned, committed couples to eventually splinter and break apart? As a clinical psychologist who has worked with hundreds of disenchanted individuals and couples, I have heard an amazing spectrum of creative explanations and rationalizations. Sometimes the triggering issues of severance seem reasonable and valid: unforgivable betrayals; unresolvable conflicts of core values; dramatic changes of behavior, temperament or personality. Other times the presenting reasons that devoted partners offer for the shattering of their intimate bonds seem not only petty, but ridiculous:

- *"All he ever does any more is sit in front of the television."*

- *"If I knew I would have to endure this much nagging, I could have just stayed home with my mother."*

- *"Try as I might, I could never convince him to vacuum the carpet in straight lines like it should be."*

- *"Before we got married she could hardly wait to get me into bed: now she has the sexual appetite of a rutabaga."*

- *"I'm not willing to stay with a man who can't even remember our anniversary after seventeen years."*

I have seen more than a few marriages deteriorate into divorce under the auspices of tubes of toothpaste being squeezed improperly, silverware being placed wrong-side-up (whichever way that might be) in the dishwasher, aggravating driving habits, room temperature disputes, overcooked meat, skirmishes over the remote control and fights about putting toilet seats down. However, after extracting the fundamental meaning of these diverse accusations and justifications, a central theme becomes clear. After boiling down their assorted complaints, what people are really saying is:

"Things just didn't turn out the way I thought they would. My partner is simply not the person I hoped they would be. Marriage isn't at all what I expected."

Whenever relational reality falls short of our expectations, hopes are dashed, resentments flourish, blame is cast and the ensuing conflicts often prove to be more than partners can bear. Faced with the harsh alternatives of sacrifice, accommodation or complete demolition and rebuilding of the relationship, the disenchanted parties, as often as not, decide to split up. The grating anger felt over "being sold a false bill of goods"—being the victim of some horrible emotional bait and switch—compels people to abandon their sinking relationship in search of something better. But the resultant disappointment, bitterness and distrust do not end simply because of separation or severance. These emotions are etched like ugly, indelible tattoos—ever-present and insidiously affecting future relationships.

Disillusion is almost always the precursor to *Dissolution*.

It is clear that there is an epidemic of disillusionment and fractured ties. In America, the national divorce rate hovers around 50% with certain counties in states such as California registering rates as high as 70%. Of the marriages that do survive, many persist solely due to factors such as economics, children, religious beliefs and the ongoing stigma of divorce. Actual estimates of genuine mutual satisfaction between marital partners range only from about 2% to 10%. It is startling to realize just how few healthy, happy relationships actually exist and endure.

But is it really possible that the durability of our love relationships falls short of our allegiance to something as impersonal as our sixty-nine dollar automobile tires? Evidently so. After all, how many of us actually go through disillusionment with our radials? How often do we drive back to the service center or garage and cry out:

"I would like to return this tire—trade it in for a new one, one that I can trust and depend on when times get hard and the road gets rough. The tire you sold me just isn't what I hoped for—it's not the tire I expected it to be."

While people do return tires due to specific defects, the divorce rate of tire owners from their roadwear constitutes a very small fraction of total sales. Goodyear, Michelin, Firestone and the like do not stay in business by disappointing customers with bad merchandise.

On the contrary, customer satisfaction is essential to their sales and profit. None of these companies could survive a 50% divorce rate.

So how do they do it? How is it that a cold, bureaucratic tire manufacturer can facilitate a successful marriage between an automobile owner and a black hunk of molded rubber—a union between driver and tire that has the probability of outlasting the sacred vows of many a devoted husband and wife?

My own recent experience of actually going out to buy a new set of tires shed some interesting light on the matter. Suddenly, the difference between how we enter into a relationship with merchandise versus how we begin our love relationships became abundantly clear.

Before venturing out to make my tire purchase, I had to determine exactly what I needed. I consulted the original owner's manual for my car and found the information on page 122. According to the manual, if I wanted to replace the original equipment, I needed to get P195/60 R15 87H Michelin MXV3 tires. After locating and selecting a tire center in the yellow pages, I went down to make my purchase. The serviceman took great pains to explain the meaning of the arcane specifications and went on to offer me a wide range of options, alternative brands, prices and service plans. After much discussion, I ended up getting the exact tires I had previously owned since they had served me well and I felt comfortable staying with a proven product.

The serviceman then carefully reviewed the terms of warranty, installation, servicing and price and gave me a comprehensive twenty page manual filled with details and guarantees. Ten minutes later I left with a credit card carbon copy, a sales receipt, a work order for installation, my extensive manual and warranty, and a general good feeling that I was getting a trusted product at a reasonable price. The terms of the transaction could not have been spelled out more clearly. I knew I was getting exactly what I needed, and I was also confident of the standing guarantee in case of any problems or in the event I was not completely satisfied. I received no special treatment—this was simply the tire dealer's standard way of doing business.

Back home, as I was filing away the paperwork from my tire purchase and marveling at the amount of detail and fine print involved, I happened to come across my marriage certificate in an adjacent folder. The contrast was astounding! My marriage certificate—the only official record documenting the most important commitment of my life—consisted of a six-by-eight-inch sheet of flimsy, white paper stating the following:

Marriage Certificate

State of Oregon
County of Marion   No. 60780

This is to certify that the undersigned, a <u>Baptist Minister,</u> *by the authority of a license bearing date the* <u>29th</u> *day of* <u>April 1974</u> *and issued by the County Clerk of the County of Marion, did on the* <u>11th</u> *day of* <u>May 1974</u> *at the* <u>Judson Baptist Church</u> *in the county and state aforesaid*

Join in Lawful Wedlock

<u>Eric Joel Cohen</u>
of the County of <u>Santa Clara</u> *and the State of* <u>California</u>
and
<u>Luanne Seymour</u>
of the County of <u>Marion</u> *and the state of* <u>Oregon.</u>

in the presence of :   *Witness my hand:*

Jill Seymour   *Robert Cahill*
                                      Minister

Todd Poulter
Witnesses

That was it. No terms, no promises, no stipulations, no guarantees, no warranties. Not even a small paragraph of fine print at the bottom. Only a terse declaration. While my tires play a very small role in my life and have little connection to my ultimate happiness, the clarity of transaction manifested in my certificate of marriage looked pathetic compared to the comprehensive documentation and understanding which accompanied my new Michelins.

Why is that we insist on hypervigilance and painstaking specificity when it comes to business deals, but resort to the most obscure cues and smoke signals when it comes to personal relationships? Every product we purchase these days comes labeled with detailed descriptions of ingredients, directions, guarantees, warnings and disclaimers. We have been educated to be assertive consumers, scrutinizing and demanding patrons backed by a legion of Better Business Bureaus, consumer advocate groups and, of course, a surfeit of attorneys ready to litigate on our behalf whenever the terms of agreement come into the slightest question.

When it comes to business, we are acutely aware of promises, expectations, loopholes and any terms involved in the exchange—and we want it all in writing. But when it comes to our personal relationships, we somehow switch into a different mode—brain-dead. Our demand for precision goes out the window and we operate as if everything will magically be understood. We fail to explicate our expectations, wants and needs because we assume that those who are emotionally close to us will intuitively know our innermost desires. We act as though our partners possess the powers of telepathic transmission, clairvoyance and omniscience.

**In personal relationships, it is not a matter
of the fine print being left out of the agreement;
it is a matter of the agreement being left out
of the communication process altogether.**

All too often, couples reach a point of exasperation and impasse because the underlying agreements of their relationship are unspecified and their assumptions about one another prove invalid. They might believe that a mutual understanding has grown between them, but in actuality, by ignoring the details and terms of their desires and needs, the door is left open for a chasm of misunderstanding.

All of us can resonate with the disappointment evidenced below by Karen and Bob.

> Bob, wearing sweatpants and a t-shirt and carrying a basketball under his arm, entered the kitchen to get his car keys. Karen, his wife, looked up from the sink where she was washing dishes.
>
> "I can't believe you're going out to play basketball again tonight and leaving me here alone with a sick baby."
>
> Bob turned to Karen and replied, "It's Tuesday night, honey. You know I have a game."
>
> "Doesn't it matter to you that your daughter is ill?" she asked with a look of dismay.
>
> "Give me a break, she has a slight cold," he shot back.
>
> Karen dried her hands angrily on a dish towel and flung it down on the counter. "It wouldn't matter if she had pneumonia, Bob. Nothing would stop you from going to your damned game."

"Why do you always have to exaggerate everything? Megan doesn't have pneumonia; she has a runny nose. But that's not the point." Bob, trying to keep his cool, reasoned with Karen, "Listen, Karen, you knew sports were important to me long before we ever got married. Why do you make an issue of it now? You even used to come to all my games. I thought you liked watching me play."

"We have other responsibilities now," Karen sighed. "You promised that after we had kids you would settle down and be home more often."

Unable to remain calm any longer, Bob shouted, "Settle down? I've already quit two teams and am down to playing once a week. I agreed to cut back on basketball, not give it up altogether. I love sports. I thought you did, too."

"Not twenty-four hours a day," Karen shot back, "If you're not out with Howie or Jim playing basketball or tennis, you're glued to ESPN. It's like Meg and I don't exist. This isn't my idea of a marriage, Bob—the only time you pay attention to us is during half-time or commercials."

Exasperated, Bob launched back, "Well, I never signed up for a life sentence of changing diapers or baby-sitting while you talk to your mother on the phone for God knows how long. What did you expect? Did you think that I was going to magically transform into Mr. Mom after the wedding ceremony? For God's sake, Karen, be realistic."

"I thought you would become a little more responsible and mature," she chided him.

"You know what, fine! I'll stay home. I won't play in the game tonight. Will that make you happy?" Bob shouted.

"No! Don't stay home because of me!" she snapped.

"Well damn it, what do you want from me, Karen?"

Karen looked up at Bob with tears starting to stream down her face. "I want you to love, honor and cherish me till death do us part—like you said you would."

"I do love you, Karen," Bob told her, "but obviously not on the terms you want."

The mutual frustration shared by Bob and Karen is in no way uncommon. They both suffer from misperceptions, discrepant expectancies and unmet needs. Their marital hopes and intentions were never clearly spelled out from the beginning nor were their conflicting values and desires ever negotiated. Both partners feel misunderstood and cheated. Both partners feel that they have made dramatic efforts to accommodate the other. However, Bob doesn't think that Karen sees or appreciates his sacrifices, and Karen likewise feels that Bob is blind to the concessions she has made. All that screams through the tumult of their frustrations is how their partner has sorely let them down.

**Broken promises lead to broken hearts—
or more accurately, *perceived* broken
promises lead to broken hearts which in
turn lead to shattered relationships.**

While business exchanges at least attempt to specify the terms of transaction, in personal relationships the underlying agreements seldom are discussed or defined. In fact, the very idea of intimate partners definitively setting forth the terms of their relationship is usually interpreted as stilted, artificial and a sign of distrust:

- *"If you really loved me, you would just know."*

- *"If I tell you what I want, you'll only be doing it because I asked."*

- *"If you really trusted me you wouldn't need an explanation."*

- *"Why can't you just be sensitive—do I always have to spell everything out?"*

It is amazing how much spontaneous intuition and magic people expect in their human relationships. Karen expected Bob to give up sports almost entirely and to settle into the domestic life she had planned. When Bob continued to play basketball and watch sports on television, she was dismayed, angry and felt betrayed, yet she didn't recognize that she wasn't betrayed by Bob's promises, but by her own expectations.

We want our partners to be sensitive and to know our deepest longings, but we don't want to be forced to express our desires openly or out loud. We feel that clarity and direct communication will somehow diminish the feeling of love that we experience from our mate. Instead of verbalizing our wants and needs—"I need you to stop and listen to me," "I would like you to take me out for my birthday," "Please make love to me"—we continually place ourselves in potential lose-lose situations by forcing our partner to read our mind and heart. If our mate fails to telepathically detect our desires, we chastise them for being insensitive or uncaring. If, because of our frustration and sense of deprivation, we finally get around to expressing what we want, then we turn on our partner and accuse them of responding to us only because we were forced to verbalize and pressure them.

In communication analysis, this bind has been termed the "be spontaneous paradox." It goes like this: *I expect you to know what I want and spontaneously give it to me without my having to ask.* Unless the recipient of this unspoken message can consistently figure out his partner's desires and execute flawlessly, he will be destined to fail and certain to disappoint his mate. Any attempts to reconcile the situation after the fact—that is, give their partner what is desired once the desire has finally been made known—will only be met with rebuttals of, *You're only doing it because I told you to.*

It is a no-win situation for both parties. Once the recipient of the message fails to accurately mind read, then his sincere attempt to later fulfill the spoken desire garners no appreciation. As for the person with the need, her overt expression, in and of itself sabotages the very experience she seeks, because, in the end, she doesn't want her partner just to respond—she wants him to *want to* respond:

- *"I don't want you to just make love to me, I want you to want to make love to me."*

- *"I don't want to tell you what to buy me for my birthday, I want you to surprise me." (But it damned well better be what I want!)*

- *"I want her to trust me so much that she never has to worry about where I am, who I'm with or what time I come home."*

- *As Karen told Bob when he offered to stay home, "No! Don't stay home because of me!"*

The idea that our partners should intuitively and spontaneously be in tune with our expectations and desires is an alluring, romantic notion, but it has no basis or correlation with reality. The fact is, each of us is a unique individual with different values, perceptions, thoughts, hopes and needs. It is common but disastrous to project our own experience onto anyone else—to presume that because we think and feel a particular way that others either will or should experience the same things. The repetitive outcry: *"I can't believe you acted like that, I would never think of doing such a thing,"* is indicative of a lethal false assumption—that somehow other people process information, experience emotions and express themselves in the same way that we do.

It's shocking how frequently I see couples in serious trouble, because one or both parties operates with the blind faith that their partners are experiencing the world exactly as they do. When this erroneous belief becomes the basis for a relationship, then the partners logically conclude that direct communication is unnecessary and can be dispensed with. Operating out of such a mind-set, we fall into the trap of believing that the terms of a relationship can remain unspoken. Instead of clear and heartfelt communication, we rely on the mystical notion that others will automatically think, feel and act as we do.

However, there is a monumental problem with leaving the details of a relationship to chance or intuition—it simply does not work in the long run. The false assumption that others will be sensitive to our unexpressed desires or accurately understand our unvoiced needs sets the stage for the perception of broken promises. Partners may believe that they are operating with a valid notion of their existing agreements, but each person may have a significantly different picture of what constitutes the covenants between them. As misperceptions manifest into conflict, both individuals end up feeling deceived and cheated.

Each person may feel in his own mind and heart that clear promises were made and agreements solidified. In the preceding vignette, Karen believed that Bob was fully committed to changing his priorities after they started a family. In her mind, his frivolous pursuit of basketball should have all but disappeared in favor of the daily demands of child rearing. But from Bob's perspective, he had more than fulfilled his promise by already drastically reducing the time he spent pursuing his passion for sports. There is no question that some understanding had been reached earlier regarding Bob's allotment of time for sports. However, since the terms of agreement were fuzzy and undeveloped, both Bob and Karen feel that they have lived up to their end of the bargain while their partner has not.

The ensuing marital debate becomes analogous to opponents in a baseball game arguing over a foul ball. One player cries foul while the other player adamantly declares that it's fair. But in the relationship, no clear foul line has ever been drawn. Each person appeals to his own sense of what is fair or foul without any predetermined chalk line. Of course, even when a clear foul line is established there can be close calls and disputes. Without any demarcation, every hit ball becomes the subject of argument and interpretation.

Before long, the battles jump from the original issue to a dispute over whose perception, memory or interpretation of the facts is right or wrong. At this point a flurry of comments may be tossed back and forth such as:

- *"I never said that."*

- *"I distinctly remember you agreeing to..."*

- *"That may be what you thought you heard, but that's not what I said."*

- *"Why are you always twisting things around?"*

The escalation usually leads to a debate over whose truth is the real truth, with both partners digging in their heels. Each person may sincerely believe that his or her version of reality is the accurate one, which inevitably leads to the conclusion that their partner is either lying or distorting the facts. If the argument escalates further, it almost becomes a battle over who is crazy (deluded, misguided) and who is sane (perceiving reality clearly).

The entire spiral of despair has now unfolded: beginning with ambiguous promises and unvoiced commitments, leading to shattered expectations and resentments, and finally disintegrating into accusations of intentional deceit or even mental impairment. The culmination of this emotional clash is a pervasive sense of unfairness. In the end, the accumulation of all the perceived inequities can leave partners feeling as though an inviolate trust has been broken which demands some form of just compensation. The result is the creation of what I term, *Emotional Debt*—the unpaid obligation between a relationship *Debtor* and a relationship *Creditor*.

Using this vocabulary, relational debtors perceive that they owe something while relational creditors believe that something is owed to them. The existing debt can emanate from positive or negative events from the distant past to the present moment. But regardless of the debt's nature, origin or duration, one or both partners consciously or unconsciously experience a sense of either owing or being owed something. The following two vignettes serve to illustrate the relational debtor/creditor concept.

As Susan put her coat on, she turned to Peter and reminded him, "Don't forget, you need to be here between noon and five to let in the phone repair man. I'm going out shopping with Alice and won't be back till about six."

"So, I'm stuck here all afternoon?" Peter asked, annoyed.

Susan buttoned her coat and sighed, "Look, I told you about my plans yesterday."

Peter stared back and said, "Well, I've got things I need to do today and your plans happen to be a real pain in the ass."

Susan rolled her eyes. "Don't make such a big deal about it. It's just one day where I get to do something that I want for a change."

Peter reddened. "One day? It seems to me that you have the whole week to do what you want while I'm out busting my butt at work trying to earn a living."

Susan finally lost her temper. "Hey," she shouted, "hold on a minute. You're the one who wanted to be the big, important attorney. I worked *my butt* off for three years waiting tables to put you through law school. I had to forfeit my scholarship to nursing school to support you back then. Do you remember that?"

"How could I forget, you'll never let me. Here it comes again—Saint Susan, the patron saint of lost scholarships," he said in a mocking voice. Susan's face reddened as Peter went on. "I don't know how you can keep throwing that in my face. My law degree has given us a great lifestyle that you benefit from as much as I do."

"You're missing the point, Peter," Susan interjected. "I really had my heart set on becoming a nurse and you took that away from me. Don't you see, your salary will never make up for that."

By definition, Susan is an emotional creditor. She perceives that Peter has not adequately repaid her for sacrificing her nursing scholarship. Her relinquishing of a nursing career and support of Peter through law school constitutes the relational debt. It makes no difference that Peter believes he has balanced off Susan's sacrifice with his substantial income. In Susan's mind, a debt persists. Her emotional sense of Peter's indebtedness places her in the role of creditor—deserving recompense for her decision to give up nursing.

The next dialogue demonstrates the emergence of a relational debtor.

> Gina stood over her father's bed in a sterile hospital room. As the doctor stood nearby making notations on her father's medical chart, Gina said firmly, "Papa, as soon as the doctor discharges you from the hospital, I'm taking you home with me."
>
> Sam, her father, argued, "Honey, you only have a one-bedroom apartment—there's no room for me there. Besides, you have yourself and Amanda to worry about."
>
> "It won't be a problem," Gina told him reassuringly. "I'll do whatever I have to. I'll make it work, Papa."
>
> The doctor interrupted their conversation, "Gina, your father needs twenty-four hour care for at least the next few months. It's just not feasible for him to stay with you. He and I have discussed it and we feel that Hamilton Gardens Nursing Home would suit him best." Seeing Gina's smile fade, the doctor added, "They can provide him with excellent care."
>
> Sam quickly added, "They've got all kinds of activities for me there, Gina. It's really the best thing for now. Maybe after I get better we can talk about living together some time. It's just not possible for you to try to take care of me while I'm like this," he said softly and patted her hand.
>
> "Look, Papa," she protested, "you need to be with family. After all you've done—raising me by yourself, college, supporting me through my divorce—I'm not going to abandon you now. That's the least I owe you."

Clearly Gina feels that she owes an enormous debt to her father. His care and support through her own troubled times have left her with a sense of indebtedness that she feels compelled to repay now that he is in a state of ill health. Since Gina perceives that she owes something back to her father, she fully meets the criteria for being a relational debtor.

Emotional Debt arises from the
perception of unequal giving or receiving.

The key word is perception. Whenever a debtor perceives that she owes something, then by definition a debt exists. In the same way, if a creditor perceives that something is owed to her, then likewise a debt is born.

Relational debts are icebergs—sometimes there is clarity and awareness of an existing debt above the waterline, but more often, the debt lies submerged beneath the surface, waiting to inflict damage whenever partners crash into it. An individual can be sailing along in a relationship through apparently calm water when, all of the sudden...she collides with the hidden debt, abruptly shattering all equilibrium. It can happen as innocently and suddenly as is demonstrated in the following exchange.

"Honey, have you seen the checkbook?" Alan asked his wife, Faye.

Faye looked up and chided him, "Listen, Mister, the way you've been spending money this month, you're not going to get your hands on another check until you start bringing home some steady income."

Alan's eyes widened in disbelief, "Whoa, where did that all come from? I just asked for the checkbook, not a lecture on my employment status. I thought we agreed it was important for me to leave the company if I was going to get my own consulting business off the ground. You knew the transition wasn't going to happen over night."

"Listen, Alan, all I know is that we're barely scraping by," she retorted. "I don't know how we're going to pay our mortgage next month. It's getting so I can't sleep at night. I am just not willing to quietly support a wide-eyed, dream chaser like my mother the martyr did. I'm not that noble, and besides, you owe me more than that."

"For God's sakes, Faye, do you think this is an easy time for me? I'm scared to death. I've been working as hard as I can to get things off the ground. I'm not your God damned father. I wish you'd get that through your head," he said angrily.

Alan thought that he was merely asking a simple question concerning the whereabouts of the checkbook, but before he knew it, he had crashed headlong into an iceberg of debt. His "innocent" question triggered a festering resentment in Faye that was rooted not only in the financial stresses of their marriage, but also in Faye's bitterness concerning her family of origin. Faye's status as a creditor—feeling that Alan owes her a certain level of financial security—is compounded by the debt which she feels that her father incurred by not being a responsible wage earner, and which forced Faye's mother to support the family.

The sudden flare up between Alan and Faye is demonstrative of how a seemingly innocuous question can spark hurts and resentments that are not always easy to untangle and make sense of. The intensity of Faye's reaction in turn triggered defensiveness and anger in Alan. In a matter of moments they entered into a rancorous dispute involving a multitude of complex issues: the couple's financial pressures, Faye's anxiety about paying the bills, Alan's stress over trying to get a new business started, Faye's deep-seated resentments about her father's failures and her mother's passive support of him, Alan's anger over being compared to Faye's father...The lid was blown off a powder keg and issues were flying in all directions.

But the picture can be brought into focus when the concepts of emotional debt are introduced. We can begin to see things in terms of Faye's perception of being owed certain debts from her father, her mother and her husband and we can begin to systematically address each debt in terms of its origin, impact, validity and resolvability. The fact that Alan may be totally unaware of Faye's perception of being a creditor does not change the reality of her resentments. The debts which she experiences exist, whether he can see them or not.

Debts arise from perceptions; and since
perceptions are not always shared, most
debts remain submerged and hidden.

CONCLUSION

Emotional debts are real. Even when they are hidden and unacknowledged, they impact relationships on a daily basis. In fact, they are often the primary underlying force which governs the quality of interaction and connection. The origins of emotional debt are frequently long-buried experiences that have bruised and violated our personal sense of fairness. The emotional debt can be either mutually acknowledged or perceived by only one party, but in either case the debt will be influential in contributing to the level of relational distress. Often times, a petty, superficial incident will ignite the emotions connected to the underlying debt, thus infusing the minor disagreement with an intensity entirely out of proportion. The incidental "facts of the case" are just the trip-wire that triggers the negative feelings tied to the unresolved emotional debt.

Due to the powerful impact that emotional debts have on relationships, the quest for debt identification and debt resolution is vital to the ongoing pursuit of a balanced union. In the chapters ahead, it will become clear that, as relational debts are uncovered, defined and resolved, partners can be free to experience the full range of satisfaction and intimacy that human relationships have to offer.

Chapter 2

JHE PLUNGE JNJO DEBJ
Origins of Relational Debt

'Twas but my tongue, 'twas not my soul that swore.
- Euripides

A WORLD OF DEBT

I am not a madman—I am neither crazed, delusional nor certifiable. In fact, it is my job to diagnose such things. I like to think of myself as intelligent, reasonable and responsible . . . but let me describe a bit of my personal financial situation and let you come to your own conclusions.

I live in a $600,000 home. I "own" this home, at least in the conventional sense that home ownership has come to be defined in our culture. On the basis of my home's value, one would think that I am wealthy, but let me put this picture into focus. First, I live in the San Francisco Bay Area. When I moved to this area a friend told me, *"This is God's country—only He can afford to live here."* The truth of these words became all too clear. The home I subsequently bought is a thirty-five-year-old, 2400-square-foot tract house that originally sold for $31,000. My wife and I purchased it from the original owners—a retired couple who felt profoundly embarrassed over the huge amount of money we were forking over for their modest dwelling.

Since my wife and I did not have $600,000 in our pockets, we did the typical thing and approached a bank for a loan. Over the past six years we have refinanced three different times and currently have a mortgage of about $430,000 on which we pay approximately $2,600 a month. We used to pay over $3,200 a month, but we applied for a new, adjustable-rate forty-year mortgage in order to bring our payments down. At the time of closing this last loan, we received a Truth-In-Lending Disclosure Statement which declared that in the year 2035 (when I am eighty-two years old) we will have paid $1,252,124.73 in principal and interest in order to fully purchase our $31,000 tract home. Let me reiterate—I am not a madman (although writing this makes me wonder). In fact, I have been told by both my accountant and financial advisor that buying my house was a very savvy move.

The point is that financial debt is something all of us have been conditioned to accept. We live with debt each day under the shadow of our country's deficit and through our own mortgages, education loans, car payments, charge accounts and credit cards. Overspending and financial debt have been called the disease of the '90s by credit counselors who try to help well-meaning spenders dig themselves out of the graves of debt which these frenetic consumers have dug for themselves.

But is it any wonder? After all, everywhere we turn, advertisers and merchandise hawkers of every ilk offer immediate gratification for no money down. *"No monthly payments until March," "0% financing," "drive now, pay later."* But too often, in the words of songwriter Tom Waitts, *"The large print giveth and the small print taketh away."* We jump at the chance to grab what we want right now and only later wake up to the dismal realities of our financial predicaments once they are beyond control. We are conditioned for such overspending early on. It is a true yet disturbing fact that my daughter actually received a letter from Mastercard offering her a $1500 line of credit when she was only seven years old!

Our programmed propensity for going into financial debt sets the stage for taking on other kinds of debts. It has become second nature for us to function as debtors and creditors in our economic lives, and this mentality carries over to our personal relationships as well. In the same way that we take on financial debts without weighing their real burden, we are also predisposed to falling into emotional debts without any awareness of doing so.

Since debt permeates our lives, it is important for us to have a clear picture of how debts are created in our relational spheres. We need to draw back the curtain to reveal the processes which work to bring emotional debts into being. Just as there are a multitude of ways that debts can be incurred financially, there are also a variety of ways that relational debts originate. A comprehensive grasp of these possibilities will prove helpful.

The Origins of Emotional Debt

Emotional debts can be created through either *positive* or *negative* events. The precipitating event, depending on whose frame of reference is examined, will determine the debtor or creditor. Since the causal event may be helpful or hurtful in substance, four basic scenarios of debt formation are possible:

1. **One party harms their partner and some form of restitution is perceived to be owed.**
   "I hurt you – I owe you."

2. **One party feels harmed by their partner and some form of just compensation is owed.**
   "You hurt me – you owe me."

3. **One party does something positive for their partner and some form of repayment is deemed necessary.**
   "I give to you – you owe me."

4. **One party receives something positive from their partner and some form of payment is owed in return.**
   "You give to me – I owe you."

Because an emotional debt is determined by the perception of *either* party involved, the four scenarios expand into eight distinct permutations of potential debt situations. The matrix shown in Table 1 illustrates the array of possibilities for debt formation.

Table 1.
Eight Possibilities Of Debt Formation

Nature of Precipitating Event	Possible Scenarios	Possibilities of Debt Perception	Perception Creates Status of:_____
		I perceive that I owe you	I am a *DEBTOR*
	"I HURT YOU-I OWE YOU"	You perceive that I owe you	You are a *CREDITOR*
NEGATIVE		I perceive that you owe me	I am a *CREDITOR*
	"YOU HURT ME-YOU OWE ME."	You perceive that you owe me	You are a *DEBTOR*
	"I GIVE TO YOU-YOU OWE ME"	I perceive that you owe me	I am a *CREDITOR*
		You perceive that you owe me	You are a *DEBTOR*
POSITIVE		I perceive that I owe you	I am a *DEBTOR*
	"YOU GIVE TO ME-YOU OWE ME."	You perceive that I owe you	You are a *CREDITOR*

In each case, it is both the nature of the precipitating event (positive or negative) and the perception of each partner that define the debt and determine which party is debtor and which party is creditor.

All of the possibilities of debt creation can be clarified and brought to life through the following series of case studies.

I HURT YOU – I OWE YOU

Negative experiences involving a sense of injury are frequent precipitators of relational debts. Whenever one person harms another in a way that leaves either party feeling that some form of restitution is owed, then by definition an emotional debt has been created. Certain debts may be perceived and acknowledged by both partners, but there are also many instances in which a debt exists only in the mind of the holder. The case of Cindy and Ron exemplifies a situation in which a negative act from the past lodges a feeling of indebtedness in the mind of only the offending party.

Cindy and Ron have been married for three years and have had their share of ups and downs. Cindy's chief complaint is that Ron never shares his feelings with her in any meaningful way and that he consistently acts in an overly accommodating manner. Ron was apparently more open and assertive earlier in their relationship, but has taken on a passive, almost fawning demeanor which is driving Cindy up a wall.

"I get so sick of his coddling and gratuitous deference that I almost want to strangle him," Cindy complained. "It's always 'whatever you want, Cindy—whatever will make you happy.' I wish for once he would tell me what he really thinks or what he really wants. I'm starting to feel like I'm married to a mirror, not a man. It's almost as if he is afraid of me or something. He never used to be this way."

Upon interviewing Ron by himself, some important facts unfolded which helped explain his behavior. Ron revealed that six months after he and Cindy were married, he ran into an old girlfriend during a business trip and ended up spending the night with her. Ron tearfully related his story:

"It was a fluke encounter. I mean, neither of us set it up or anything, but we both had too much to drink and before I knew it we were at her hotel room. I knew it was wrong, but I slept with her anyway. I've never told Cindy. I think it would crush her and I really do love her and want our marriage to work. I've tried as hard as I can to repay her for my stupid mistake, but the guilt hasn't gone away. I don't know if it ever will."

Ron is a prime example of a relational debtor. A one-night-stand with his old girlfriend has created a perceived debt which hangs over his marriage like a black cloud. He has been trying to pay off the transgression ever since, but to no avail. The irony in this situation is that not only is Cindy totally unaware of the existing debt, but that Ron's efforts to please and appease her have ended up becoming the very core of her frustration. In a sense, Ron's solution has become his problem. His veiled attempts to repay a hidden debt have only served to irritate his beloved spouse and in turn intensify his own feelings of guilt, betrayal and ongoing inadequacy. Ron's intentions are sincere, but since the debt remains undisclosed and his chosen form of repayment (appeasement) is unacceptable, he is unable to liquidate his debt or escape its ongoing impact. Even though the damaging debt is perceived by only one party, Cindy's aggravation festers, Ron's guilt persists and the foundations of the relationship have slowly eroded.

> *Debts* **do not have to be mutually acknowledged in order for them to have powerful influences on relational patterns.**

The case of Ron and Cindy is illustrative of a situation in which the offending party (Ron) is the sole perceiver of the debt. He has committed what he considers to be a hurtful act and it is his perception which defines both the debt and his role as debtor.

There are also situations, however, where it is the *offended* party rather than the *offending* party who determines the debt situation. The case of Simon and his older brother Dave is a good example.

> Simon (age thirteen) and his brother Dave (sixteen) were left alone at home for the weekend while their parents went to a relative's wedding. On Saturday, Simon was using Dave's camera and accidentally dropped it into the swimming pool. Dave had given his younger brother permission to use the expensive 35mm camera, but was furious with his brother for what he felt to be gross negligence. When their parents returned home, Dave demanded that Simon's savings account be used to provide him with a replacement camera. Simon felt that his brother's solution was unfair.
>
> Simon pleaded with his father, "He said I could use the camera, Dad. I didn't mean to drop it into the pool. I'm sorry I did, but why should I have to buy him a new one with the money I was using to save up for a bike? It was an accident. I didn't mean to do it. He didn't have to loan me the camera in the first place."

Apart from the fact that Dave's and Simon's parents have a sticky situation over which to render a parental decision, the vignette provides a good example of an offended creditor (Dave) who feels that the harm he has incurred (a waterlogged camera) warrants a debt settlement. In this case, the offending party (Simon) does admit that he has indeed caused harm to his brother, but because the harm was due to an accident, Simon neither acknowledges the debt nor is willing to assume the role as debtor. Nevertheless, Dave's perception is, in and of itself, sufficient to establish the debt and perpetuate its impact.

It takes only one partner's viewpoint for a relational debt to arise. It is analogous to how "marriage problems" can be defined by the unilateral perception of either party. In marriage, if one or the other partner feels there is an existing problem, then, by definition, a marital problem does exist. It makes no difference whether the other party sees, acknowledges or agrees with the issue. This same principle holds true for emotional debts. In the above example, Simon's denial of the debt in no way prevents the debt from arising or from affecting the relationship with his brother.

The case of Dave and Simon is also valuable in that it illustrates how the model of relational debt is applicable to all types of relationships, not just adult love relationships. Here, Dave's sense of debt is directed towards his brother. Thus far, our focus has been on marital and love relationships, because the debt model initially evolved from counseling couples. But the concepts of emotional debt extend to all types of relationships.

Emotional Debts can occur in any
relationship—spouses, love-mates, family
relations, peers, co-workers and friends.

YOU HURT ME – YOU OWE ME

All of us experience certain disappointments and emotional pain in our long-term relationships. But if the hurt gives rise to a sense that some form of recompense is owed, then a debt is formed. Again, the created debt may be understood and acknowledged by both parties, or the debt may be unilaterally harbored. In the following case, the existing debt is clearly apparent to both partners involved.

> Laura and Ben have been married for twenty-seven years and have three grown children. When their middle child Randy was seventeen, he was arrested for drunk driving. Ben, who grew up with an abusive, alcoholic father,

always took a hard line with his kids about alcohol use in general.

"I told all three kids from the time they were in grade school that they could do what they wanted after they turned twenty-one and left home," he explained. "But I would not tolerate any drinking as long as they lived under my roof."

When the police called Randy's parents after the arrest, Ben made it clear that he did not want his son back in his house. Randy was held in jail for two days until he was arraigned and finally released to his parents' custody. Ben refused to speak to Randy over the ensuing months and eventually his son left home to live with an uncle.

Laura expressed her sadness over the rift between her husband and son and over the heartbreak of having to watch her only son Randy move out.

"I understand how hurt and angry Ben was," Laura said, "but it tore me apart to see him treat Randy like that. I tried to tell Ben how I felt at the time, but he refused to listen. He acted as though my opinion and my love for my own son carried no weight. The more I tried to reason with Ben, the more he withdrew. Now I feel like I have lost my son and my husband as well. I have to admit, I've held a grudge against Ben ever since. Things have smoothed out a little with time, but I don't know if I can ever get over what Ben did to Randy . . . or to me. He knows I still resent him but he has never budged an inch. I'm not sure what it would take for me to forgive him at this point."

Laura clearly defines herself as an injured party deserving some form of restitution. Ben is well aware of Laura's feelings—he has heard her articulate them for many years. He knows full well that Laura harbors a debt over his harsh treatment and rejection of their son, but Ben's awareness of this debt has done nothing to motivate him toward any conciliatory action. Ben still believes he was right to deal with Randy as he did and sees no need to apologize or offer any form of payment for his wife's perceived debt. Ben's unyielding perspective and discrepant values (or, according to Laura, "his stubborn pride and unyielding arrogance") block any possibility for repayment, even though the debt has been voiced. Ben clearly understands that the debt persists in Laura's mind, but he adamantly refuses to grant it any merit.

**Even when one party refuses to accept
a debt's validity, that debt will continue
to plague the relationship.**

In couple's counseling, Laura confessed that she had attempted through a multitude of direct and passive-aggressive ways to extract some form of payment from Ben for his rejection of Randy. After ventilating her anger time and again, she withdrew affection, abandoned household chores and eventually took a weekend job in order to be away from the house and away from her husband. Ben knew full well why she was punishing him, but his refusal to acknowledge the legitimacy of the debt and his failure to offer any meaningful settlement caused a bitter stalemate.

Ben's concession to participate in couple's counseling was solely based on Laura's threats of a divorce. Despite his reluctance and resistance, Ben showed up for the sessions and gave strong voice to his sense of righteous indignation against his son as well as the total lack of support he had felt from his wife. During several intense meetings, both parties spewed out their resentments with no yielding on either side. It became clear that the future of their marriage hinged on the willingness of both Ben and Laura to each move from an entrenched position and to try to enter into an understanding of the other's intense feelings. Without some kind of concession, divorce seemed imminent.

Finally, faced with the stark reality of losing the person he loved, Ben was able to step out of his own blind rage enough to grant Laura her right to see things differently. He began to accept the reality that, whether he agreed with Laura or not about the precipitating incident, her perception of debt could no longer be ignored if the marriage was to be salvaged. His eventual willingness to acknowledge her pain and anger, even though he still viewed the situation from an opposite perspective, led to an open discussion of what Laura needed in order to achieve some form of resolution. Once Ben made this shift towards acknowledgment, Laura slowly softened and the threads of connection were painstakingly restored. Ben's validation of Laura's hurt, and the affirmation of her sense of being owed, proved to be the springboard for reconciliation and reunion.

I GIVE TO YOU – YOU OWE ME

Just as debts can be incurred from negative actions, a sense of indebtedness can also crystallize through incidents which are positive in nature. A partner may extend a simple favor, offer a gift or make a significant sacrifice which results in the feeling that something is now owed to her in return. Again, it may be either the perception of the giver or the receiver of the benevolent act that determines the debt.

In the case of Joan and her sister Sarah, it is the giver who ends up feeling owed. Here, the person performing a kind deed has placed herself in the position of emotional creditor by virtue of the behavior which she herself initiated.

Joan's best friend, Doris, lived out of state and recently suffered a serious stroke. Joan flew out to help Doris, expecting to be with her for only seven to ten days. Joan's sister, Sarah, offered to take Joan's children so that Joan would be free to leave and care for Doris.

"I knew how badly Joan wanted to be with Doris," Sarah explained. "They are as close as two friends can be. After Doris lost her husband two years ago, she has been pretty isolated. There are really no other family members in the picture, so I understood Joan's need to go. Anyway, I was more than happy to take my niece and nephew for a week or so. I knew Joan felt guilty about leaving the kids with me, but I pushed her onto a plane and assured her she was doing the right thing."

Joan flew out to Milwaukee, thankful for her sister's support. Unfortunately, unexpected complications with Doris's recovery required Joan to stay an additional three weeks.

Joan voiced her emotional predicament. "Sarah told me to take as much time as I needed, but I knew she was reaching her limit. I could hear it in her voice each time I called. I felt trapped. Doris needed me by her side, and I had no choice but to count on Sarah to understand. I didn't know what else I could do."

Sarah admitted that her patience was strained after a month of covering for her sister. "Four weeks with two extra kids in the house started to grate on me. Bob and I also had to cancel a weekend trip we had planned for our anniversary. I didn't have the heart to tell Joan, but I was really upset that Bob and I had to forfeit our plans in order to cover for her. I can't help it, but I really feel like Joan owes me something back for all I did. Of course, I would never admit it to her—after all, I was the one who offered to watch the kids. But I really do feel like I was forced to go above and beyond my sisterly obligation. Now I feel like I can't win. Either I keep my mouth shut and carry my resentment inside, or I selfishly speak my mind and risk ruining my relationship with my sister."

Sarah's guilt over feeling that her sister owes her something in no way changes the reality of the existing debt. Sarah may wish that she didn't feel a need for reciprocation, but the fact is she does. Denying her true emotion does not discharge the debt. Neither does trying to rationalize the debt away by thinking such things as:

- *"It's selfish for me to want something back in return."*

- *"I should be glad to help whenever I can without always expecting some kind of reward."*

- *"After all, she is my sister."*

Denial and rationalization may temporarily postpone problems, but eventually, suppressed feelings will manifest directly or indirectly. Sarah can attempt to talk herself out of feeling owed or she can try to bury these emotions. But ultimately, such internalization can yield a plethora of physical, emotional and relational symptoms ranging from headaches, stomach upset, high blood pressure, anxiety, depression, passive-aggressive behavior and relational withdrawal.

Conflict avoidance—the decision not to voice the perceived debt—is never a lasting cure or solution. Instead, failure of a debtor or creditor to declare their perceived debt only serves to prolong the debt's impact. Sarah's option of verbalizing the perceived debt to her sister, and attempting a frank discussion of how the debt can be settled, is ultimately her best choice for both her own health and the health of their relationship. Resolution, though it can seem risky and frightening, is always preferable to repression. By finding an appropriate setting and implementing a non-accusatory mode of expression, the resolution of Sarah's perceived debt can become a less threatening proposition. Then, the opportunity for harmonious settlement is heightened.

YOU GIVE TO ME – I OWE YOU

A debt can also be created when one individual is on the receiving end of a kind gesture, resulting in the beneficiary feeling a need to extend some form of compensation. The person in the role of giver may have no expectation or desire for recompense, but the receiver, nevertheless, feels compelled or obligated to offer something in return.

Such unilateral creation of debt was exemplified by one of my cases. Following the successful completion of her therapy, Eve, one of my clients, wrote me the following letter:

Dear Dr. Cohen,

So much has happened since the kids and I left Bruce and moved back to Arizona to be with my parents. The divorce was finalized last May and I was awarded sole custody of the children. The court ordered Bruce to go through an alcohol program before any visitation would be granted, but he refused and we have not heard from him since.

The kids have adjusted well to all of us living with my parents. They still miss their dad, but none of us miss his hostility or abuse. As for me, I have been working part-time and finally found the courage to take the writing course I always promised myself. I'm starting to believe that my dream of writing children's books doesn't have to remain a fantasy.

I am enclosing a check as a token of my deep appreciation for all you have done for me. I recently came into some money and wanted to try to repay you for the support and guidance you gave me during the most trying time of my life. Please accept it as my gift to you for helping me get my life back. It feels good to be a whole person again.

With sincere thanks,

Eve

Inside the envelope was a sizable check that my professional code of ethics would not allow me to accept. Eve had already paid me in full for the entire course of her therapy. Our exchange was complete and even—I had performed my job and had been fully compensated for my work. I certainly had no sense that Eve owed me anything else for my services. But regardless of my own feelings, Eve clearly felt in debt. I wrote her back the following note:

Dear Eve,

It was so good to receive your letter and hear how well things have turned out. Your generous check over- whelmed me. I can't tell you how rewarding it is to feel so appreciated. However, the ethical code which governs my profession prohibits me from accepting your gift.

I have thought it over carefully and would like to propose an alternative to your monetary gift. First, I would ask that you keep me on your Christmas list and send me an update each year about you and the kids. I don't often get to hear about my clients after they complete therapy and I would love to keep track of your ongoing progress. Secondly, I would like to request a signed copy of the first children's book you get published. Trust me, you could repay me in no better way than to honor these requests.

Thanks again for your thoughtfulness and for taking the time to write. Give my best to the children.

With fondness and best wishes for continued happiness,

Eric

I knew that simply refusing her check would still leave Eve feeling unbalanced in our relationship. She had a need to extend some tangible form of repayment to me even though I held no thought of additional compensation. With the debt model in mind, I knew that the best solution would be to request something from Eve that would be ethical and acceptable from my end and that would still satisfy Eve's need to give something significant to me.

After receiving my letter, Eve wrote back a week later and happily accepted my proposal. Both of us were gratified to have her perceived debt fully settled in this manner. Now, I get a wonderful card each year at Christmas time, and her autographed book, though not yet a published reality, has a cherished spot on my bookshelf awaiting its arrival.

Thus far, we have explored a variety of ways in which emotional debts can be incurred through either the positive or negative acts of a debtor or creditor. It is also possible, however, for certain debts to emerge independent of any direct acts by either partner. For instance, one way debts can form involves an exaggerated attitude of **entitlement** which certain ego-centric individuals bring to their relationships. This category of debt warrants a closer look.

ENTITLEMENT: I AM DESERVING – YOU OWE ME

Most of us have encountered individuals with an inflated sense of entitlement—people who feel that the world owes them something simply because they are alive. Terms such as "self-centered," "narcissistic," "ego-maniac" and "spoiled rotten" are frequently used to label such personalities. Their predominant mode of operating is that their needs should always take precedence over the needs of others. Their sense of entitlement carries with it a sense of universal ownership— *"What's mine is mine and what's yours is mine if and when I want it"*—which seems justified by a pervasive notion that the world owes them everything.

Often such feelings are rooted in a childhood of overindulgence—a silver spoon upbringing. Children who are lavished with attention and gifts and who are sheltered from the normal responsibilities and consequences of life are programmed to expect immediate gratification without effort. The expectation is that the world will continue to freely bestow gifts upon them just as their parents did.

For others, a sense of entitlement can emerge as the by-product of emotional deprivation and narcissistic development. Certain people who must overcome an environment of neglect, paucity or even abuse may develop a sense of deserving a better life in reaction to the lack of attention or absence of tangible goodies never received. In this case, the individual truly feels that the world owes them a debt for the harsh treatment or deprivation which they had to endure earlier in life.

Regardless of the etiology, entitlement is a major factor in relational conflict. Just how the mind-set of entitlement manifests itself as emotional debt can be seen in the following conversation.

"Take a look at this ad, Ray. Maiden Cruises is offering a thirty percent discount on their trips to Hawaii. Wouldn't it be great to just pick up and go for a week? I'm sure my mother would take the kids," Tracy told her husband.

"Sure sounds nice, honey, but that's still about seventy percent more than we can afford," Ray answered.

Tracy pouted and whined, "If it were up to you, we would never go anywhere. Why don't you ever think we deserve a nice vacation?"

"It's not a question of what we deserve," Ray explained, "it's a question of what we can afford. Look, Tracy, I run a hardware store, not a diamond mine. Besides, I can't just pick up and leave for a week. You don't seem to understand what it takes to keep a business running. It's not just the cost of going on a vacation. It costs us money every day that I'm away from the store."

"Well, something's got to change. I'm tired of living on a shoe string and having everyone else we know buying big homes and taking exotic trips," Tracy responded angrily.

"Listen," he scowled. "I work hard to make a living and allow you to stay home with the kids like you wanted. No one is stopping you from getting a job if you're feeling so deprived. You could pick up some part-time work downtown and start saving towards a nice trip. Why should I have to carry the whole financial burden? You act as if I owe you the world."

"We've been through that a hundred times. I need to be home with the children," she shot back. "I don't expect everything, but I certainly deserve a lot more than what I'm getting around here."

Tracy's belief that she is owed a certain lifestyle does not stem from any positive or negative act that she or Ray has initiated. Her status as a creditor is entirely based on her own conception that somehow she is owed a certain standard of living. Like those ensnared in adolescence—the quintessential stage of entitlement—Tracy expects everything to be given to her without the necessity of earning it. Because Ray happens to be closest in proximity, he serves as her lightning rod for every feeling of entitlement. Tracy's demands for gratification discharge themselves like bolts of negative energy onto Ray.

Her expectation is that he must provide everything she wants without question.

> **Entitlement is always underscored by Debt—**
> *"You owe me." "They owe me."*
> *"The world owes me." "...and by God,*
> *somebody is going to pay!"*

Individuals governed by entitlement usually are baffled by their partner's failure to share in their belief system. Entitled individuals expect everyone else to intuitively know their needs and desires and to react accordingly:

- *"Of course that's what I expect."*

- *"Everybody knows that."*

- *"How could you not understand something so obvious?"*

- *"It's just common sense!"*

> **Unfortunately, sense, beliefs, values**
> **and perceptions are rarely *common*.**

Tracy's line of argument with Ray is entirely based on her perception of what she feels she deserves. Ray's pragmatic concerns about time and money, or his suggestion that Tracy generate additional income herself, are all disregarded in favor of her expectation for immediate fulfillment. Tracy can blame Ray's stinginess, his limited income, or even his lack of adventure, but in the end, it is really her own sense of entitlement which creates in her the feeling that she is owed something.

INHERITED DEBTS:
THEY OWED ME – NOW YOU OWE ME

Just as financial debts can be assigned from one party to another, emotional debts can be unknowingly transferred. In a business situation, a creditor will seek out a secondary payer if the original party has not made good on the deal. For instance, if my daughter failed to make her car payments, I, as the responsible co-signer, would be held accountable for the loan. Of course, the fact that I am a willing co-signer explicitly carries the risk of such responsibility.

But in many relationships, individuals inherit debts which they never knew existed and never agreed to take on. Until the existence of past debts came to the surface, Miles and Barbara were stuck in a morass of hurt and confusion. Their situation, though complicated by intense trauma, was able to be clarified through the discovery of an enormous inherited debt.

Miles and Barbara had been married eight months when they finally sought help for their sexual problems. Both partners had been raised in conservative Christian homes, so they had chosen to refrain from sexual intercourse prior to marriage. Barbara had seemed reserved, but the couple exchanged affections openly (hugs, kisses, hand-holding) during their courtship. But after the wedding, Barbara began to shun all advances. Miles convinced his wife to start therapy with him because his level of frustration over their non-existent sex life had reached a breaking point.

Miles gave voice to his frustration, "Every time I make any kind of advance, Barbara freezes up and pulls away. I've tried to be gentle and understanding, but she simply refuses to allow me to initiate any sort of affection. She treats me like I'm a leper or some kind of sexual deviant. Believe me, Doctor, I have never treated her in a way to warrant this kind of rejection."

After a number of private sessions with Barbara, she revealed a part of her past that clearly was responsible for her difficulties with sex.

"My brother was ten and I was six when he started fondling me. Things just escalated from there. It went on for about six months before he finally stopped. He used to come up to my room and force me to do things whenever Mom left the house. He threatened to hurt me if I ever told anyone. He even tried to convince me that I was the one who wanted him to . . . to touch me. Being violated like that was horrible, but I think what I hated most were his threats and intimidation. I remember, even as a six-year-old, telling myself that I would never let any boy treat me like that ever again.

"When I fell in love with Miles, I had to work hard to be affectionate at first. But later, it felt good to let him hold me and be close. I guess it was safe because I knew things wouldn't go any further back then. I know it sounds stupid now, but I never thought about the reality of actually having sex after the wedding. I just blocked it out.

"But once the wedding night arrived, it was like I woke up and the terror hit me. All those horrible feelings about my brother flooded into my head and I panicked every time the possibility of sex came up. I couldn't help it, I treated Miles horribly. I just couldn't tolerate him touching me any more. I didn't have the courage to tell Miles about what my brother had done to me. I feel horrible for how I've treated my husband, but I just can't get past my revulsion and fear."

The complexity of this case is intensified by the trauma of incest. Clearly, Barbara has a significant need for personal healing: working through her rage over her brother's dominance, violation and betrayal; restoration of her capacity for trust and physical intimacy; and balancing the charged issues of control and power.

However, despite the intricacy of the case, the consideration of emotional debt is immensely helpful in focusing on many of the relational dynamics. Barbara, the creditor, feels that a huge debt is owed to her because of her brother's past sexual abuse. The debt has never been acknowledged or repaid by her brother, so now the debt has been transferred to her husband, Miles.

Miles has unknowingly inherited this debt from his brother-in-law. Without any awareness, the debt Barbara incurred from her brother has now been transferred to her husband. Miles, and probably Barbara as well, are both ignorant of the existing debt, Miles' status as an assigned debtor and Barbara's position as the creditor. However, by implementing the simple conceptual framework of relational debt, both Barbara and Miles can begin to understand their relationship from a new perspective and can start to deal with such essential questions as:

- *How has Barbara's past victimization impacted her marriage?*

- *Is it fair or reasonable to expect Miles to provide some form of compensation?*

- Is Miles willing to take on the debt, and if so, is there any way he can effectively resolve it?

- What will it take for Barbara to have this debt settled? Is it even possible for such a debt to be repaid?

A common language and an open discussion of these issues provide a workable format for Miles and Barbara to confront the obstacles to intimacy that have plagued their marriage and their sexual relationship. The resolution of their problems will not occur easily or quickly, but the identification of past relational debt can be of tremendous value in bringing a new understanding to their situation, facilitating their process of renewal. Barbara can begin to focus more directly on the debt instigated by her brother's abuse and its impact on her current marital struggles, and Miles can gain relief from the sense of personal rejection he has experienced while this debt has remained submerged. A new level of understanding can become the platform for genuine healing.

SELF-DEBT: I FAIL – I OWE

The final type of debt formation to be considered is *Self-Debt*. Each of us, in a sense, lives in relationship to ourselves and to our own image of success. We make promises, commitments and bargains with ourselves based on our life goals and desires. These guiding objectives are generally the product of parental expectations, societal norms, peer pressures and other external influences. But as we formulate and internalize our personal standards and aspirations for success and achievement, we must contend with the potential of either living up to our expectations or falling short. When we fail to reach our self-imposed milestones, we risk the possibility of becoming indebted to ourselves as seen in the following example.

George was the oldest of four children and clearly the brightest and most ambitious. He grew up in a small, working-class town and excelled academically at a level way beyond his peers. When he came for counseling, George nostalgically described his early successes and then grew visibly depressed as his current situation came to light.

"I was valedictorian of my small high school and a straight-A student through college. Everything came very easily to me, especially math and science. I completed a degree in engineering and then applied to business school since I had strong ambitions to start my own company and make a lot of money. I went to Harvard, but it proved to be a rude awakening. I went from the peak of being exceptional to the valley of mediocrity.

"After graduating, I held to my goal of starting my own company and becoming a millionaire by age thirty-five. Things just haven't gone my way, though. I'm now thirty-eight and still struggling to succeed. I tried to get two businesses off the ground but could never generate enough venture capital to ever give them a chance. I lost most of my savings as well as a substantial amount of cash which family and friends invested.

"I was forced to go back to a salaried position in a large corporation by default. Everything seems so mundane at this point. I promised myself I wouldn't end up like this, but here I am. I've totally let myself down."

George's sense of failure needs to be viewed in light of the fact that he is a high-level managing engineer earning a six-figure salary. He also has a stable marriage, two healthy children and a supportive network of friends. Yet George still defines his life as a waste and battles ongoing feelings of depression, guilt and existential despair.

**Failing to live up to our personal goals
creates a *Self-Debt* characterized by shame
and disappointment.**

George needs to face the debt he has imposed on himself and find some means of settlement if he is to overcome his emotional state of depression. He may need to renegotiate his original expectation of becoming a millionaire and having his own company if he is to discharge his self-debt. In George's case, the resolution of his debt is essential to achieving a new level of self-acceptance and a positive self-image.

George's situation is rooted in issues of career and financial success. But self-debt can be the by-product of a myriad of other self-imposed expectations: social status of marital partner, athletic prowess, spiritual development, and moral integrity. Regardless of the nature of expectation, self-debt is always characterized by feelings of self-deprecation, guilt and frustration. Self-debt is the precursor to despondency and personality breakdown and therefore must be acknowledged and resolved before a devastating downward spiral of self-hatred begins.

CONCLUSION

We have looked at the variety of ways that emotional debts can form. We have seen how debts can evolve from either the positive or negative actions of one partner or the other. For instance, emotional debts may be created when one partner is given help or support and, in turn, feels as though he owes some form of repayment to the giver. In other examples, we have seen how an emotional creditor can be created when one party harms another with the result that the offended partner feels that he or she is owed compensation for the harm suffered. We have also explored how unprovoked debt can arise through the unilateral sense of entitlement one person brings to the relationship or how a debt can be transferred from one party to another. In these instances, neither positive nor negative action by either partner is involved. Finally, we have explored how debt can be incurred when an individual fails to live up to his own expectations and the ensuing sense of failure leads to self-debt. With a comprehensive understanding of how emotional debts are formed, we can move ahead to examine common types of emotional debtors and creditors.

ASSESSING YOUR EMOTIONAL DEBTOR AND EMOTIONAL CREDITOR STYLE

In the next two chapters, we will be exploring different types of emotional debtors and emotional creditors. As a prelude to this discussion we have provided a self-assessment checklist which will help you determine which categories of debtors and creditors describe you best. You can use this tool to assess yourself or you can use it as an insight into someone else.

Read each statement carefully and check *every* sentence that accurately portrays how you view yourself and the world around you. If the statement is true for you, check it. Although this inventory is not a standardized test, it will help you identify personality trends that lead to becoming an emotional debtor or creditor.

IDENTIFY YOUR EMOTIONAL DEBTOR OR CREDITOR TYPE
A SELF-ASSESSMENT INVENTORY

INSTRUCTIONS: Read each item carefully and place a check mark next to those which you feel are descriptive of you. When you have finished, go to the Tally Sheet at the end to record and interpret results.

B ___ I will say almost anything to avoid conflict.

A ___ I try to figure out what others expect of me and do it the best I can.

B ___ Others complain about my lack of follow-through.

C ___ I make sure that I get my way almost all of the time.

E ___ I am not satisfied with anything less than perfection.

I ___ People complain about my pouting, but it works.

G ___ I feel cheated when I am denied what I want.

I ___ When someone hurts my feelings, I go out of my way to make sure they know.

J ___ I believe in a tit-for-tat approach to relationships.

I ___ I have a better chance of getting what I want if I get someone else to feel sorry for me.

H ___ I don't have sympathy for weak people who get taken advantage of.

J ___ When I do something for another person, I expect something in return.

I ___ I know that I frequently make other people feel guilty.

H ___ Getting my way with others is like a game to me.

J ___ Relationships work best when everything is kept balanced in terms of equal giving and receiving.

F ___ More things go wrong in my life than in the lives of others.

J ___ I do not like to do more for someone else than they do for me.

I ___ I am good at putting on an act of being emotionally hurt as a means of getting what I want from others.

C ___ I don't mind becoming loud or abrasive when issues are important to me.

A ___ I focus on what pleases others and tend to put myself last.

D ___ I often offend others without realizing it until later.

J ___ It is essential for me to have things exactly even in a relationship.

G ___ I deserve and intend to get more out of life than others.

F ___ People don't realize how hard I have it.

J ___ If I share a meal at a restaurant with others, I like to divide the bill equally.

H ___ It's *what* you get from others that matters, not *how* you get it.

I ___ The easiest way to get what I want is to use guilt as leverage.

G ___ Others complain about my being self-centered.

F ___ I often feel like a "victim."

C ___ I have little or no respect for most people.

F ___ I see the world as a very unfair place.

G ___ I see myself as superior and therefore warrant special treatment.

J ___ I expect reciprocation for any favors that I do.

G ___ I deserve to get what I want when I want it.

F ___ I feel powerless to deal with life's hardships.

H ___ It is easy to spot someone I can manipulate for my own purposes.

I ___ If I can get someone to feel sorry for me, then it is easy to get what I want from them.

G ___ Others should defer to my needs and desires.

H ___ Once someone feels obliged to me, I can easily get what I want from them.

A ___ I prefer not having the responsibility of making the decision.

C   ___   For me, the end often does justify the means.

E   ___   Others complain about my high expectations.

B   ___   I avoid conflict by giving assurances I am unable to keep.

C   ___   People often see me as a "bully."

D   ___   I am not very good in social situations.

D   ___   I often "put my foot in my mouth" by saying insensitive things.

A   ___   I'll do almost anything to make people like me.

B   ___   I often tell people what I think they want to hear.

D   ___   People often see me as socially inept.

E   ___   If something is not "done right" it tends to drive me crazy.

D   ___   I feel that others are often embarrassed to be with me in public.

A   ___   I see myself as inferior to those around me.

D   ___   I see myself as a "misfit" and a "klutz."

C   ___   I have little patience for the ideas of others.

A   ___   I am in constant fear of disappointing others.

C   ___   What matters most to me is getting my way.

D   ___   I make others feel uneasy by my own awkwardness.

E   ___   I strive to make everything as perfect as I can.

A   ___   Others often take advantage of me.

B   ___   I tend to make commitments that I know I can't keep.

E   ___   I have little patience for my own mistakes.

A   ___   No matter how much I do for others, it never feels like enough.

C   ___   Others see me as demanding and overbearing.

E   ___   People see me as judgmental and exacting.

B   ___   I promise more than I am able to deliver.

E   ___   Others don't like to work with me because of my high expectations.

A   ___   I am very afraid of disappointing others.

B   ___   People often complain that I am late.

C   ___   I see others as weak and incompetent.

D   ___   Often I don't understand why people get upset with me.

A   ___   I will do almost anything to avoid criticism.

D   ___   I am not sensitive to how I hurt or embarrass others.

B   ___   I over-extend myself by committing to unrealistic goals.

B   ___   I am not very good at sticking to a schedule.

E   ___   I expect a great deal of myself and feel bad when I fall short.

D ___   I do not understand or care about social conventions and etiquette.

E ___   Nothing is ever good enough for me.

F ___   I often feel targeted and taken advantage of.

G ___   Life owes me a lot.

H ___   It is easy for me to exploit the weaknesses of others.

J ___   I do not like someone else to do more for me than I do in return.

F ___   I resent the bad things that happen to me in life.

I ___   Most of my requests are indirect and colored with guilt-inducing messages.

H ___   I fulfill my own needs by "using" other people.

F ___   I often say to myself, "why me?"

J ___   I like to divide chores and responsibilities evenly with my partner.

F ___   Others don't seem to have lives as hard as mine.

G ___   There are certain things in life that are simply owed to me.

I ___   I keep track of every favor someone owes me.

G ___   People accuse me of being "spoiled" and expecting too much.

H ___   I am not afraid to take advantage of someone else.

J ___   People see me as "keeping score" in relationships.

H ___   I don't mind using and then discarding people.

F ___   You just have to "put up" with life and take what comes to you.

G ___   I feel like a "special" person who deserves more than others.

H ___   I pick people to relate to that I know I can use in some way or another.

I ___   I know exactly what to say to make others feel bad so that they will do what I want them to do.

I ___   Sometimes I'll sulk to get what I want.

G ___   Others complain about my disregard for their opinions.

EMOTIONAL DEBTOR AND CREDITOR TYPE
TALLY SHEET

Instructions: Tally the number of times you checked each capital letter on the left of each statement. Record the number of checks below. Refer to the Scale to help interpret your tendencies as an emotional debtor and creditor.

DEBTOR TYPE		CREDITOR TYPE	
A ＿＿ Deficit Doormat		F ＿＿ Resentful Mark	
B ＿＿ False Advertiser		G ＿＿ Entitleist	
C ＿＿ Robber Baron		H ＿＿ Emotional Loan Shark	
D ＿＿ Blunderer		I ＿＿ Guilt Extortionist	
E ＿＿ Perfectionist		J ＿＿ Bean Counter	

SCALE

0 to 3 responses   You have some mild tendencies in the direction of this type of emotional debtor or creditor.

4 to 6 responses   You have strong characteristics of this type of emotional debtor or creditor. This may be problematic to you or others.

more than 7   You fit this profile of an emotional debtor or creditor and need to consider some changes.

Chapter 3

HABITUAL DEBTORS
Portraits of People Who Owe

Now that you have broken through the wall with your head,
what will you do in the neighboring cell?
- S. J. Lec

We all know individuals who seem to make an unending series of unwise investments, whose every financial endeavor results in their falling further in the hole. The day they buy a stock inevitably marks the all time high; and they can't pull the trigger to sell until it bottoms out. Their idea of a can't miss opportunity could be anything from a multi-level marketing scheme to an overpriced time-share.

Just as there are certain people who exercise poor judgment in their business transactions and are prone to financial debt, in the realm of human interaction, there are likewise individuals with a strong propensity for going into relational debt. This is not to say that any of us are immune from becoming relational debtors, but the personality make-up of some people dramatically predisposes them to incurring debts.

Some people are like *Debt Magnets*,
accumulating *Debts* in virtually all situations.

Most of us have encountered the five most common types of debtors at one time or another. Descriptions and examples of each will help unveil their patterns and make-up.

TYPE 1. DEFICIT DOORMATS:
INSOLVENT, SELFLESS MARTYRS

The Deficit Doormat is the kind of person to whom you could serve a rancid egg salad sandwich and not only would he or she eat it all, but this individual would politely ask you for the recipe. Doormats are people who seem to have "WELCOME" written across their chests, inviting anyone and everyone to walk all over them twenty-four hours a day.

Deficit Doormats **feel it is their duty**
to absorb all the dirt and debris that
their abusers care to deposit.

We all know people who look at themselves as God's gift to the world—Deficit Doormats are the exact opposite, possessing little or no concept of what they deserve in life. They have no trouble attributing rights to others, but when it comes to their own lives, they function as though they are unworthy of any consideration or respect. Such individuals take on the role of self-sacrificing martyrs—always putting their needs beneath the needs of others. Because of this pattern, they always function in deficit modes—as though they inherently owe others because of their own inferiority. Doormats are easily recognizable by their deferent, accommodating and submissive behavior and by their lack of any genuine identity. They constantly use phrases such as:

- *"It really doesn't matter to me one way or the other."*

- *"Whatever you decide is perfectly all right."*

- *"I'm happy as long as everyone else is happy."*

- *"Don't worry about me, I'll be just fine."*

Doormats behave from the presumption that they owe everything to everyone all the time.

For *Deficit Doormats*, **their constant**
attempt to pay off imagined debts is their
<u>**problem**</u>, **not their** <u>**solution**</u>.

The development of the Doormat personality can evolve in different ways. The first avenue is through a process of observation and internalization. If an individual grows up with role models who exemplify or value selfless surrender, that person will likely adopt similar patterns of behavior. Many people are taught to embrace extreme self-sacrifice as a worthy goal. An ethic of submission and accommodation is upheld in many religious spheres as well as certain secular value systems. In such environments, individuals become Doormats by attempting to emulate a standard that they have been taught. Selflessly "doing unto others" is the sacred golden calf of their devotion, and anything short of total sacrifice is experienced as insensitive, rude and self-serving.

Doormats can also develop in situations where feelings of self-deprecation or worthlessness are instilled from critical outside forces. If children grow up in environments in which they are continually demeaned, criticized, dominated or ridiculed, it is difficult for them to form any kind of positive identity. If parents are abusive, explosive, neglectful, overly rigid or suffering from their own pathology (mental illness, alcoholism, etc.), children will often internalize the message, "something must be wrong with *me*." Children in these situations are likely to feel defective or "less than" because they are treated as though their thoughts and feelings count for little or nothing. These children may develop hypervigilance and hypersensitivity to their parents' moods and demands in order to defensively anticipate responses as a means of avoiding more criticism or abuse. Eventually, children forced into self-deprecating roles learn to ignore their own feelings and instead become more sensitive to the needs and desires of those around them. As these tendencies are carried into later life, the patterns of Deficit Doormat personalities become entrenched. As adults, Doormats continue to defer and respond to the requirements of everyone else, with little or no sense of their own personal rights or values.

A third environment in which the Deficit syndrome develops is a family experience plagued by overprotection and emotional smothering. In such circumstances, the parents treat the developing child as though he or she were a piece of fragile china—never allowing autonomous decision-making or risk-taking. The protective parents are usually operating out of a sincere concern for the child's welfare, but the child ends up internalizing quite different messages: *You are helpless; you are incapable and inadequate; you should fear the world and try to avoid danger at every turn.* Self-confidence and self-esteem never have a chance to germinate because no faith in the child is ever instilled. Like the child who is a product of abusive parents, overprotected children end up seeing themselves as defective and inferior.

The case of Douglas is typical of this personality formation and the resulting propensity for a life of relational debt.

Douglas is a thirty-two-year-old computer programmer referred to therapy by his internist who was treating him for gastroenteritis and irritable bowel syndrome. Douglas's physician believed that his patient's physical symptoms were primarily due to his inability to deal with stress. However, it became clear from Douglas's description of his current life and past history that most of his stress was rooted in extreme social anxiety.

"Whenever I'm with other people, I feel myself get nervous and tighten up. I am always trying to figure out what everyone expects of me—then I do my best to act it out. My mind races a hundred miles an hour. I find myself searching for every little detail and cue as to how other people are thinking and feeling. It's like when other people enter the room, my radar turns on and I become flooded with panic. I live in constant fear that somehow other people will be disappointed or angry with me if I don't do everything just right. It's such a relief for me to be alone and not have to worry about all of this."

Douglas grew up as an only child living with his mother and grandmother. His father died in an auto accident when Douglas was two and his mother constantly dreaded that something would happen to her son.

"She drove me to and from school every day. She picked out my clothes, told me which classes to take, never let me play sports and pretty much ran my life until I left for college. Even then she begged me to stay home and attend the nearby community college, but by that point I knew I had to get away.

"Whenever I try to disagree with her she goes to pieces. I've never been able to deal with her when she breaks down like that. I feel like I immediately turn seven years old again. She makes me feel so guilty and weak . . . and ashamed of myself. Mother still nags at me to put on a sweater, slow down when I'm driving, eat my vegetables . . . Sometimes I wish she were dead."

Douglas went on to describe how his relationships in general replicate this pattern of incurring emotional debt and trying to repay it. He finds himself constantly trying to please others as a means of avoiding their potential criticism or disappointment. The result is not only his painful physical symptoms (constipation, colon spasms, and a developing stomach ulcer), but also a debilitating anxiety rooted in his pervasive feeling of being in debt to others.

Like many Deficit Doormats, Douglas lives out his entire life under the shadow of unending debt. Because he sees himself as less than others, all of his relationships are colored by his impulse to address their needs and concerns rather than his own. It is essential to understand that for relational Doormats who feel extreme indebtedness, the solution to the problem does not involve paying off debts. When debts are bottomless and pervasive, no amount of repayment can ever fill the void.

Functioning as a debtor in all relationships—trying to repay an infinite deficit—is akin to bailing out a sinking canoe with a bucket full of holes. The more furious the bailing, the more spillage of water back into the boat. Bailing faster is not the answer; the drowning Doormat is still destined to sink ever lower.

Like the futile bailer, Deficit Doormats need to go through a fundamental change of approach. Trying ever harder to achieve full repayment will never get them out of debt. Instead, Doormats require the development of their distinct identity, self-esteem and a healthy sense of personal entitlement. Such a transformation in self-image can be a difficult and long-term process, but without a genuine shift in perspective and behavior, the Deficit Doormat will be destined to a hollow life of fear and appeasement.

TYPE 2. FALSE ADVERTISERS: PLACATERS WHO FAIL TO DELIVER

As stated earlier, emotional debts can evolve from either debtors' perceptions of owing something or from the presumptions of creditors that something is owed to them. The debts of Doormats are clearly based on unilaterally seeing themselves as owing others, even though others rarely share in this perception. On the other hand, False

Advertisers not only feel in debt themselves but also leave a wake of disgruntled creditors in their path.

How many of us have ordered a piece of furniture with a promise of delivery in just four weeks, only to be on the phone two months later angrily demanding our merchandise. Even though the salesperson knew full well that complications in manufacturing and shipping nearly always result in lengthy delays, they still promised the standard four weeks in an attempt to make the sale and keep us happy. Such False Advertisers may be well-meaning in their initial promises, but are inevitably swamped under by the realities of life which they fail to consider. Once their promises prove hollow, these placaters are genuinely embarrassed and offer up a stream of profuse apologies. But rest assured, the next customer through the door will still hear the same four-week guarantee.

In the sphere of personal relationships, the False Advertiser is a person who avoids conflict by deflecting others with gratuitous promises. Relational False Advertisers will promise anything and act in the most ingratiating manner as a means of keeping the waters calm. They commonly offer phrases like:

- *"Don't worry, I can take care of it."*

- *"Sure, no problem."*

- *"I'll have it for you first thing in the morning."*

- *"Trust me."*

False Advertisers **are the used car salesmen in the showroom of life.**

In their relationships, False Advertisers do their best to tell others exactly what they want to hear—even when the Advertiser senses that it is nearly impossible to make good on his promises. As long as the other person departs with the hope of satisfaction, the Advertiser is relieved from having to deal with any immediate problem.

The *False Advertiser* is always poised to put off until tomorrow any potential conflict of today.

The roots of such empty promising often lie in a childhood of extreme turmoil. If an individual grows up in an environment saturated with belligerence and argument, they often resort to coping mechanisms of avoidance and distraction. They may take on a mediating role of peacekeeper, attempting to maintain an atmosphere of quiet and calm through intuitive anticipation. In a dysfunctional family system, such behavior is adaptive and protective—if a child can learn to detect when her drunk father is about to explode and lash out, she can take pre-emptive defensive measures to stay out of his range. But once a person is conditioned to avoid and accommodate, she tends to carry the same behavior patterns into all future relationships—even when such a response is unnecessary and even destructive.

Carol's situation clearly portrays the False Advertiser pattern.

Carol is a thirty-one-year-old, highly successful realtor, who sought therapy because of a relational problem. She is attractive, energetic and highly personable, but presents a history of one failed intimate relationship after another. Her current boyfriend, Paul, accompanied her to the first session and explained his discontentment with her patterns of unreliability.

"Carol is a wonderful person, and I love her a lot, but it's gotten to the point where I feel like I can't trust anything she says. I don't mean her faithfulness or anything like that . . . it's just that she is always overextending herself in unrealistic ways. She's never on time; she's always changing our plans at the last minute; she's constantly promising to call or take care of something and then never does. She always seems to have a valid excuse—I don't think she is trying to be malicious. But after a while I started to feel like a second class citizen. Carol and I have talked about marriage, but I'm not willing to stay in a relationship with someone who promises the world and never delivers."

Carol admitted to the accuracy of Paul's criticisms and explained, "He's right. It's not that I lie or try to deceive him, but I am terrible at following through. I always mean what I tell him, but I guess I tend to promise too much. It's the same way at work—I'm always running late, getting behind in my paperwork and making commitments I can't fulfill. I get away with it with my clients because they usually like me and somehow I manage to get things to work out in the end. I've always been good at keeping my clients happy. Paul was incredibly tolerant at first, but his patience has run out and now he gets furious with me. I can't blame him. I've run out of excuses."

Carol's family history helped to shed light on her pattern of over-promising. Her mother was emotionally volatile and at times physically abusive. Carol's passive father traveled a great deal and provided little buffer to her mother's explosions even when he was home. Carol's mother fought constantly with her husband and his passivity only fueled her fire. Carol hated the yelling and screaming and would do anything to pacify her mother and protect herself and her father. She became highly skilled in this role at an early age and carried the behavior into her adult life. It was a functional defensive strategy in her pathological family, but has proved extremely destructive in her love relationship with Paul.

False Advertisers often suffer from the same low self-esteem as Deficit Doormats and can likewise play out the roles of debtors without any hope of redemption. But it does not end there. Their irresponsible tendency to commit to more than they can deliver ultimately leads to debt in the minds of those they disappoint. People on the receiving end get annoyed, distrustful and soon become creditors demanding payment against the ledger of broken promises. Carol has disappointed Paul so many times that he now feels entitled to not only the fulfillment of old pledges but even further restitution.

Unpaid debts are eventually compounded by the creditor's demand for additional compensation—punitive damages for pain and suffering.

In order to stop accumulating debt, False Advertisers must introduce a novel concept to their repertoire of responses—quite simply, they must learn when to say "No." In order to rebuild trust, Advertisers must prove their credibility and manifest integrity through the consistent fulfillment of each and every new commitment they make. False Advertisers can be rehabilitated, but it requires diligent attention to liquidating existing debts and scrupulously abstaining from the creation of new ones.

TYPE 3. ROBBER BARONS:
BULLIES EXPLOITING THEIR WAY INTO DEBT

In the late nineteenth century, prior to anti-trust laws and securities regulations, the American economy was substantially controlled by a small band of greedy industrialists who used any means available to extract financial gain. Known as "Robber Barons," these opportunists exploited every means—legal and otherwise—to defeat their competition and increase their own wealth.

Using similar tactics as those of their financial forebears, emotional Robber Barons are arrogant, rigid controllers who aggressively charge toward their own goals with total disregard for any damage they may inflict on others in the process. Robber Barons are either oblivious to the emotional carnage they leave in their wake or they simply don't care. Their sole agenda is to have everything go their way, and, as far as they are concerned, any means—no matter how loud, abrasive, humiliating or threatening—justifies this end.

The *Robber Baron's* mode of operation is:
"My Way or the Highway."

What distinguishes Robber Barons as creators of debt is that, regardless of their own abusive behavior, they never feel like they owe anything to anyone. But there is always a toxic residue of debt left behind in the minds of their decimated victims. The debt of the Robber Baron is unilaterally held by those who have been run over. It is the flattened victims who harbor resentment and desire restitution for the offenses they have suffered—even though the Robber Baron is oblivious to the notion that any debt exists. Even if the offending Robber Baron proffers an off-handed apology, his contrition is short-lived and he will soon revert to his pulverizing style.

Emotional *Robber Barons* are debtors, not
in their *own* minds, but in the minds of the
creditors they have abusively created.

When dealing with Robber Barons, you either hop aboard their bandwagon or clear out of their paths. They are not interested in what your opinion is or how you feel about an issue. The only perspective that counts is their own, and once they have made up their minds and set their courses, they are almost impossible to stop or redirect. Robber Barons effectively intimidate others by bellowing:

- *"I don't really care how you feel, this is the way we are going to do it."*

- *"If I wanted your opinion, I'd ask for it."*

- *"If you don't like it, you know where the door is."*

- *"That's the stupidest thing I've ever heard."*

Emotional Robber Barons intuitively take advantage of the fact that there are more passive, conflict-avoidant people in the world than there are assertive individuals who refuse to be run over. Thus, Robber Barons not only get their way, but they also tend to achieve positions of leadership which legitimize an even more commanding platform of power. Many figures of authority have implemented a Robber Baron's style in their rise to power. They often are very bright, articulate, charismatic individuals, highly competent in their field of endeavor.

**The problem with *Robber Barons*
is not their effectiveness; it is the manner
in which they alienate everyone around them.**

The case of Kenneth is a good illustration of the emotional Robber Baron profile.

> Kenneth is the vice-president of operations at a large aerospace company. At forty-two years of age, he is the youngest person in the company's history to rise to such a level. He has a reputation with upper management for being a bright, hard-nosed rising star who can motivate his team and run an efficient plant. When Kenneth is given a task or a deadline, he delivers. His performance record is stellar, but effective execution is the basis of his problem.
>
> Recently, a potential harassment charge was brought to the company's president by the Human Resource Department. A manager who reported directly to Kenneth complained to Personnel of "inappropriate language, threats, and belittlement" by his superior. Kenneth had thrown a tirade (as well as a clipboard) because of a missed deadline. The manager involved was unwilling to absorb Kenneth's bullying rage. No

formal charges of harassment had previously been filed against Kenneth, but his personnel record had dozens of complaints by other workers about his abrasive style and temper. The immediate threat of legal action forced the company's president to intervene. Part of the intervention required a psychological evaluation of Kenneth and ongoing counseling as needed.

Kenneth's life history was consistent with his current behavior. He grew up the eldest of three sons under the tyranny of a rigid, overbearing father. His passive mother continually yielded to his father's authoritative control. Kenneth aligned himself with his father and masterfully learned how to dominate his mother early on. When his father was at work, Kenneth got his way by throwing temper tantrums that manipulated his mother into conceding to everything he wanted. As a youngster in school, he pushed teachers to the limit with loud back-talking and he controlled his peers through both verbal and physical intimidation. As people around him yielded to his tantrums and bullying, Kenneth's behavior was reinforced and an emotional Robber Baron was born. The fact that Kenneth was disliked by nearly everyone never seemed to bother him. Like his father, Kenneth was much more interested in wielding his own power and getting his way than he was with winning the affection or acceptance of those around him.

Robber Barons **are fueled by a need for control; they are not out to win popularity contests.**

Robber Barons become relational debtors by virtue of the emotional fallout they produce. Often they have a hard time understanding why others react so negatively to their behavior—Robber Barons tend to see others as too "sensitive," "weak" or "thin-skinned" rather than labeling their own behavior as abusive or inappropriate.

Rehabilitation of a Robber Baron requires settling up with the injured parties who seek not only a change in the Robber Baron's approach to relationships but also some form of emotional restitution. Robber Barons are highly resistant to change since they are reticent to give up their power and dominance. They have little motivation for addressing the relational problems they produce because their needs for close relationships are always secondary to their desires for control. Their pursuit of change is almost always a product of someone else's upset and insistence. Nevertheless, change and transformation are possible if the Robber Baron is willing to acknowledge his damaging patterns and work diligently towards fairer and more compassionate ways of interacting.

Turning a *Robber Baron* into a
kind philanthropist is no small feat.

TYPE 4. BLUNDERERS: NAIVE TOE-CRUNCHERS STUMBLING INTO DEBT

The Blunderer is a much more sympathetic character than the Robber Baron, even though his or her mode of creating debt is quite similar. Blunderers incur debt as their behavior disappoints, upsets, offends, embarrasses or irritates others. Unlike Robber Barons, Blunderers are apt to readily acknowledge and feel responsible for the impact of their behavior—often feeling guilty, ashamed and repentant. But their propensity to blunder repeatedly and to make insensitive *faux pas* perpetuates a pattern of debt.

In the world of business, the Blunderer might be the brilliant software designer who is normally ensconced in his isolated cubical. Upon being invited by the president of the company to present his latest programming innovation to a group of prospective venture capitalists, the Blundering technoid arrives in a pair of plaid shorts, manages to knock over the slide projector and culminates his performance by thoughtlessly insulting his audience with an inappropriate joke. After the aghast audience files out of the room, the embarrassed Blunderer turns to the company president and weakly says, "I hope I didn't screw things up too much."

Relational Blunderers tend to function in social spheres the way a hippopotamus might waddle through a pottery shop. They are awkward and unaware of the environment around them, oblivious to the norms and conventions that govern social situations.

Blunderers are not deliberate or
malicious in the havoc they wreak;
they simply are out of touch.

Their hearts and intentions are often good, but their behavior is usually abysmal. Blunderers' naïve insensitivity and thoughtlessness can be heard in the types of comments they are apt to blurt out:

- *"I'm sorry, I really thought you were pregnant."*

- *"What's wrong with a vacuum cleaner for your birth-day?"*

- *"Is that a hairpiece you're wearing? It looks so real."*

- *"OOPS . . . Some Spray and Wash should get that right out."*

Tolerance for the Blunderer only goes so far. While his ineptitude may initially seem harmless and even endearing, his graceless buffoonery eventually takes its toll. Embarrassed sufferers become increasingly annoyed and significant emotional debts can accrue. The case of Jessica and Jeremy provides an eloquent example of the emotional debt that a Blunderer incurs.

Jessica and Jeremy had been married for a little over two years when Jessica insisted they go to marriage counseling. Jessica, a twenty-six-year-old dental assistant, painted a picture of her discontent.

"Jeremy is basically a really sweet guy. He reminds me of an innocent child much of the time in his honesty and unpretentious manner. The problem is that he seems to be in another world. He's always preoccupied and never seems to really listen to other people. He'll ask me about something that I just explained a minute earlier. He'll also come out with some of the most off-the-wall comments you've ever heard. It can be extremely embarrassing when we're with other people. It's gotten to the point where I'm a nervous wreck in public, always cringing at what he might say next. I'm a very social person, but I've reached the point of not wanting to go out any place with Jeremy. It's just as well, he never takes me places anyway. He'd rather be home glued to the television or his computer.

"I'm so exasperated now over the parade of past incidents that I'm finding it harder and harder to be forgiving anymore. Somehow I need to get over the past, but something has got to change now as well, or I don't think we will make it."

When Jeremy was asked how he felt about what his wife's description of his personal foibles and the impact these deficits had on their relationship, his response seemed to sum it all up, "What do you mean I never take you anywhere, Jessica?—we're here aren't we?..."

Jeremy is obviously an etiquette nightmare and his unintentional blundering has created a real rift in the marriage. Jessica's compounding mortification and resentment have reached the point where she now feels that Jeremy owes her something back for all of the blunders she has endured. Jeremy went on to admit that he was not the most sensitive person in the world, but that he never had any intentions of hurting Jessica. He was willing to continue in counseling, read self-help books, take communication classes or do whatever was necessary to preserve their marriage.

Jessica felt she could relinquish her position as a creditor if Jeremy stuck with therapy and agreed to take her out once a week on a "real" date. Jeremy was more than happy to comply and actually made significant progress at becoming more attuned to his wife's needs. A basic communication class at the local junior college and some coaching from a personal enhancement specialist helped Jeremy develop both new skills and new sensitivities.

There were still those awkward moments when Jeremy's foot needed to be surgically removed from his mouth, but Jessica was more tolerant of these incidents given the sincere efforts toward improvement that Jeremy put forth. Their weekly dates and Jeremy's ongoing progress helped to offset the debts of the past and allow Jessica to re-embrace the relationship with renewed energy and motivation.

TYPE 5. PERFECTIONISTS: INSATIABLE DEBT TRAPS

The last category of relational debtors we will discuss is the Perfectionist—obsessive, exacting individuals who are continually falling short of the unrealistic goals and standards they set for themselves. Perfectionists are plagued by a compulsive drive for control over their environment. Their sense of well-being is derived from the achievement of flawless excellence, which they define in a way that makes such an accomplishment next to impossible.

> ***Perfectionists*** **are cursed by their need to scale**
> **heights always just beyond their reach.**

When they do succeed at any given task or endeavor, Perfectionists discount their accomplishments and immediately refocus on other areas in which they are still coming up short. They discredit themselves by saying things like:

- *"It wasn't that difficult after all."*

- *"The first part went okay, but there's so much left to do."*

- *"A real expert would have done it in a fraction of the time."*

- *"I still could have done a better job."*

> **Nothing is ever good enough for**
> **the *Perfectionist*—they are ensnared in**
> **one "no-win" proposition after another.**

There are two kinds of Perfectionists: the *Ordinary* Perfectionist and the *Ornery* Perfectionist. The Ordinary Perfectionist is the person who feels that nothing he does is ever sufficient. The Ornery Perfectionist equally endorses his own inadequacy, but additionally feels that nothing anybody else does measures up either. Ornery Perfectionists impose the same impossible standards on others which they impose on themselves. They are intolerant of everyone's mistakes and shortcomings and air their displeasure openly.

- *"How could you do such shoddy work?"*

- *"Any job worth doing is worth doing well."*

- *"You should be ashamed of yourself."*

- *"The poor quality of your work is only surpassed by its delinquency."*

Perfectionists continually criticize other people in the same way that they castigate themselves. They approach life with an extremely negative view—always expecting the next screw-up at every turn.

The discontentment of the Ornery Perfectionist infects those around them. Their biting, judgmental proclamations leave others feeling dejected, demoralized and angry. A child may show her Perfectionistic parent a near perfect report card, only to have that parent criticize the lone B+. A hard-working salesman may bring home a large bonus check to his wife, only to have her complain about how meager his base salary is. Of course, the size of the check or the student's grade point average is not the issue. The fact is, nothing ever truly satisfies the Perfectionist. There is always another mountain to climb or some greater improvement to make. The case of Julie and her mother Victoria is a good example of the relational consequences a Perfectionist exacts.

When Julie was sixteen years old she confided in a school counselor about her eating disorder. Julie went on to describe a three-year history of bingeing, purging and laxative abuse. She had the typical traits of bulimia—a distorted image of her body, a regimen of compulsive exercise, extremely low self-esteem and a compensatory drive for perfectionism. Much of her behavior seemed to be the product of her tangled and unhappy relationship with her perfectionist mother, Victoria. According to Julie, her mother's exacting need for control had proven too much to bear.

"I feel like I am a glove and she is the hand inside, guiding all of my actions—only I am the one who constantly gets blamed for anything that goes wrong. It doesn't matter what I do or how hard I try. The slightest mistake and she's all over me, yelling how I can never do anything right, how I am lazy and will never amount to much.

"Its gotten to the point where I hate everything about me. I hate my hair. I hate how I look, and most of all, I hate how fat I am. My friends tell me that I'm too skinny, but when I look in the mirror all I can see is an ugly, pudgy mess. I'm so afraid of ending up like my obese mother. She's always yelling at me to not get fat, but all she ever buys is junk food and candy. I don't understand her at all.

"I don't think anything I do will ever make her happy or proud of me. It's gotten to the point where I've quit trying. It's not like I get in trouble like some kids I know. I don't do drugs or drink and I am on the honor roll at school, but none of that seems to count. As far as Mom is concerned I'm a total failure. I just want to get out on my own as soon as possible—away from her."

Julie's resentment has accumulated over her entire life. As it turns out, Julie's mother, Victoria, herself grew up with a dominating, perfectionistic mother. Victoria stewed in resentment for the treatment she had received during her own childhood, but was blind to the ways in which she re-enacted the same damaging pattern with her own daughter. Victoria clearly saw herself as a creditor in relationship to her own mother—Victoria felt that a tremendous debt was owed to her for the abuse she had to endure. Unfortunately, Victoria displayed no awareness of the debt which she was unconsciously creating in her own daughter. Julie viewed herself as a deserving creditor and her outrage was magnified by Victoria's blind adherence to a demeaning and overbearing style of parenting.

**The pathology of one generation
is often visited upon the next.**

Ornery Perfectionists such as Victoria and Victoria's mother create debt in much the same manner as Robber Barons. Their hurtful conduct injures and infects those around them, and festering debt quickly mounts. The Ornery Perfectionist may or may not be conscious of the impact of her actions, but debt accrues nonetheless. Awareness and acknowledgment of the damage and the debt are the essential first steps towards restitution for these debtors.

Ordinary Perfectionists are more akin to Deficit Doormats in their roles as debtors. Because Ordinary Perfectionists always perceive themselves as failing or falling short, they operate in a continual state of debt. Nothing they do is ever good enough by their own standards and so they feel in constant debt to themselves. They clearly meet the criteria for Self-debtors. Like Deficit Doormats, Ordinary Perfectionists can never resolve their positions as debtors by trying to pay off their debts to themselves. Rather, a fundamental shift is needed in their attitudes and standards for success if they are ever to relinquish their sense of failure and self-hatred.

The *Perfectionist's* efforts to pay off debts will always be perceived as falling short, like everything else they do.

A vicious cycle ensnares Ordinary Perfectionists: they aim at unblemished success, fall short of their standards, feel in debt to themselves, then try harder as a means of repaying the debt, fall short again, their sense of debt increases . . . and the pattern goes on *ad infinitum*. As with the Deficit Doormat, trying harder to settle debt is no solution for the Perfectionist. If the Perfectionist is committed to redefining her notion of what constitutes success, the pattern can be broken—but the process will be long, hard and, of course, always far from perfect.

CONCLUSION

Our list of habitual debtors is in no way comprehensive, but it does highlight certain behavioral dynamics which lead to debt formation. Most of us can see aspects of each debtor type within our own personalities since the characteristics described always exist in degrees. We all may falsely advertise or blunder or behave as Robber Barons from time to time, even though our entire personality is not limited to a single mode of expression. In the same way that universal psychological symptoms manifest in all of us at one time or another—each of us gets depressed, anxious, fearful—debtor characteristics show up in each of us as well. Awareness of these patterns can be a pragmatic first step in bringing to light the ways in which emotional debts are created. By understanding debt dynamics and reflecting on our personality traits and communication styles, we can strive not only to detect debts but also to work towards their prevention and resolution.

Chapter 4

CHRONIC CREDITORS
Perpetual Claimants for Repayment

The human species, according to the best theory I
can form of it, is composed of two distinct races,
the men who borrow and the men who lend.
- Charles Lamb

Just as certain individuals are predisposed to going into debt, others have propensities for becoming creditors. Their nature lends itself (pun intended) to continually placing them in the position of being owed something. Like the habitual debtors that we encountered in the last chapter, the menagerie of chronic creditors encompasses a wide range of personalities. A glimpse into the world of these perpetual repayment claimants will surely strum chords of recognition as we observe traits that we not only see in others, but also experience ourselves.

TYPE 1. RESENTFUL MARKS:
TRAFFICKERS IN MISFORTUNE

During the Depression era, wandering hobos roamed the countryside in search of opportunities for handouts and charitable care. Whenever these vagabonds discovered a particularly generous donor, they would traditionally carve a symbol ("mark") on the doorpost, signifying that household as a target for easy pickings. The term soon took on a more generalized meaning to denote anyone with a naïve predisposition for being taken advantage of. Although he implemented a different nomenclature, P.T. Barnum was quick to point out that in this world, "there is a sucker born every minute."

Whereas Deficit Doormats have "WELCOME" written across their chests, the chests of Resentful Marks are etched with Bull's Eyes. These chronic victims are the constant targets of mishap, ill fortune, poor treatment and abuse. They often refer to themselves as "jinxed," "unlucky" or "doomed." From the outside, their pattern of progressive tragedy may seem coincidental, but Resentful Marks unknowingly set the stage for their condition by self-sabotage, poor judgment and a naïve refusal to learn from previous mistakes. They are the kind of people who will re-fill a punctured car tire with air and then wonder why it went flat again—all the while continuing to bemoan fate's harsh treatment of their automotive exploits.

Resentful Marks **use their victimization as a rationale for taking absolutely no responsibility for their actions.**

As long as they can hold on to the victim role, Resentful Marks can buffer themselves against any blame or responsibility for the misfortunes they suffer. Resentful Marks constantly utter phrases such as:

- *"What did I ever do to deserve this?"*

- *"Do other people always have to be so cruel?"*

- *"Why can't something good ever happen to me?"*

- *"The world is such an unfair place."*

- *"Why me?"*

Marks perceive themselves as defenseless and powerless—as though life is governed by malicious external forces which pursue them like homing devices of heat seeking missiles. Marks have ongoing paranoia about how the misfortunes of the world intentionally zero in on them. There is no sense of personal power, self-determination or control. Instead, life to the Mark seems like a wild roller coaster ride in which he or she is helplessly strapped into the seat.

Marks passively go along for the terrifying ordeal with no sense of being able to steer, slow down or even jump off. Their passive life is simply a blind transit along a perilous track toward an ominous and unknown destination.

Resentful Marks tiptoe through the minefield
of life with their hands tightly clasped over
their eyes, ever fearful that their next step
will trigger a devastating explosion.

When confronted by genuine hardships or real obstacles, Marks become paralyzed and despairing since they do not believe they have the inner resources to effectively combat problems. The only solutions they see are forbearance and suffering with the hollow hope that eventually "things will get better."

However, deep within the core of the Resentful Mark, the whips and scorns of life are not merely tolerated or shrugged off. A simmering sense of injustice brews into a righteous desire for restitution for the bitter unfairness they have had to endure. The accumulation of resentment in the heart of the Mark translates into a covert demand for just compensation. The case of Esther is a classic illustration of how a Resentful Mark becomes a creditor.

Esther is a seventy-two-year-old woman who was referred to counseling following the death of her husband Joseph. Joseph had suffered for years from dementia and Esther had done her best to care for him at home. Esther herself appeared to have a long term history of depression although she had never been diagnosed as such. Her approach to life was extremely passive and fatalistic. She bemoaned her situation with deep sighs and words of despair.

"Things have never been easy for me, Doctor. My parents were poor immigrants who came to America and struggled to provide for us. When my father did achieve some success in his business, it was wiped out during the Depression. We lost everything. I left home at eighteen and went from one menial job to another until I met Joseph. We married and had three children, but it was a constant financial struggle. Joseph wouldn't allow me to work and his own job turned out to be a dead end. I tried to manage the best I could. Every time we started to get ahead, even a little bit, something else would happen—the car would break down, one of the kids would get sick, my parents would need help . . . I am not a strong person, Doctor, and there were many times I felt like I couldn't go on and face another crisis. But what could I do?

"After Joseph got sick, things just got worse and worse. My kids are all scattered around the country with their own families and worries, so I tried my best to take care of their father all by myself. I cooked, cleaned up after him, bathed him and tried to make him as comfortable as I could. But after a while it got to the point where he didn't even know who I was.

"Now Joseph is dead, God rest his soul . . . so what's going to happen to me now? Who's going to take care of me? I wish just once the Lord would make something nice happen for me. Don't you think I deserve it after all He's put me through?"

Esther had clearly endured her share of hardships, but her powerless approach to life certainly has contributed to both her past misfortune and her ongoing depression. Esther's despair is embedded in her feelings of unfairness and resentment for all of the bad cards that life has dealt her. She perceives that life, or God or somebody owes her something for all of the pain she has suffered.

And so, Esther, the Resentful Mark, is also Esther the creditor, hoping, praying and crying out for fate to repay its enormous debt to her. But, like all Resentful Marks, Esther has no impulse to take an active part in pursuing any realistic source of repayment. Instead, she will sulk in her misfortune and continue to tread in the depthless pool of her hopelessness and sense of victimization. And if by chance another person were to wander into her life—a replacement for her deceased husband—most assuredly he would discover the "mark" left behind.

TYPE 2. ENTITLEISTS: EVERYONE OWES THEM

Entitleists, like Deficit Doormats, function in the world with warped expectations and distorted notions of what they deserve. But whereas Doormats perceive themselves as having no personal rights, Entitleists seize upon the narcissistic notion that the world exists solely for their own gratification.

Entitleists **have an aura of royalty—as though their inherent make-up places them above the common masses.**

The Entitleist can be generous and benevolent, but more often than not there is a snobbish and impudent air to his or her manner. Entitleists can be heard making decrees such as:

- *"You'll just have to wait until I'm ready."*

- *"I expected better than this."*

- *"No, I want the one that you have."*

- *"I'm in a hurry—you don't mind if I go ahead, do you?"*

Entitleists live by their own set of unidirectional, self-serving rules—rules which they believe pertain to themselves but not others. They embrace such principles as:

- *All people are equal—but some are more equal than others.*

- *What's mine is mine and what's yours is up for grabs.*

- *The Golden Rule: he who has the gold, rules.*

- *What's good for the goose doesn't have a thing to do with the gander.*

Since Entitleists believe everything is owed to them by everybody, they are, by definition, perpetual creditors. Their status as creditors is based on their own presumptions rather than on any external circumstances.

Entitleists **believe everything is owed to them—not because of any overt acts, but simply by virtue of being alive.**

The story of Charles ("Please don't call me Chuck") exemplifies the concept of the Entitleist.

Anita and Charles sought marital counseling after a bitter dispute over the fact that Anita had taken a part-time job against her husband's wishes. Anita had been a mother and homemaker for over twenty years, but now wanted to expand her horizons. Charles was adamant that his wife remain at home. He voiced his position with the air of authority that typified his general manner.

"There's absolutely no reason for her to work. We don't need the income and I can't afford to have things fall apart around the house while Anita's off selling cosmetics or whatever it is she's planning to do. Anita's job has always been to keep things running smoothly at home and to be available for entertaining my business associates and clients. She knows that my career requires her support and hospitality. She knew that when we got married. You just don't get to a position like I have without a certain amount of involvement and sacrifice from your spouse. It's got to be a team effort. I can't believe that after I've worked this hard to get this far Anita would pull the rug out from under me like this. You've got to talk some sense into her, Doctor."

Anita had quite a different perspective. She explained, "You don't understand, Charles, I want to work. I need to finally have a life of my own."

Charles quickly interrupted, "That's not the point, Anita. It's my career that we're talking about. I need you at home and that's that."

Anita could no longer contain her anger and shouted, "Where do you get off thinking that you're so high and mighty. I'm sick of living my life like some kind of second-class citizen. I'm not your servant, Charles. You've always done whatever you pleased and gotten what you've wanted. I've gone along with it for twenty-two years, but I'm putting my foot down right now.

"It was different when the kids were still home, but now I need something more. You don't seem to understand that. You're so wrapped up in your own world and so worried about maintaining your image that you just don't realize the rest of us have lives, too.

"I'm sick of feeling like I owe you the world. I'm taking this job whether you likes it or not, *Chuck*. And that's that!"

Charles sat upright and responded in a tone of controlled anger, "I've never heard you speak to me this way before, and I certainly am not going to tolerate it now."

Charles clearly feels entitled to having his game plan for life carried out without question or challenge. But Anita has reached her limit. She refuses to continue functioning as a Deficit Doormat under the foot of Charles' entitleistic demands. In Charles' narcissistic way of thinking, *his* wife is an extension of himself and thus should be available to meet *his* needs, execute *his* agenda and facilitate *his* goals and objectives. But Anita's tolerance for playing out this role of submissive helpmate has come to an end. With the departure of her children from the home and a deeply felt need to reestablish her own identity, Anita is finally willing to say, "NO!" She will no longer pay tribute to Sir Charles by honoring his detailed scroll of edicts. However, since Charles is cemented into his mind-set of entitlement, he remains blind to Anita's needs and is loath to relinquish any part of his status as the deserving creditor. The result is a marital stand-off in which neither partner is willing to budge an inch.

Entitleists must ultimately weigh the cost of their world view and self-perceptions. If they are ever to experience meaningful relationships with true partners, they must set aside their superior status and attribute rights and respect to their partners. If they ever want to find genuine satisfaction in relationships, Entitleists must come to see the futility caused by their quest for ceaseless payment.

Charles may have valid issues concerning how his relationship with Anita is being transformed without his consent. It may be true that Anita had willingly accepted the role of housewife/entertainer as her contribution to the marriage—Charles obviously feels that the ground rules were clear all along until his disgruntled wife wanted to change everything in midstream. But ultimately, Charles needs to value Anita as a person in her own right—with her own feelings, needs and entitlements.

If he is unable to embrace his wife as a person and maintains his entitleistic notion that she continues to owe him anything he wants, he will likely lose Anita. If Anita declares emotional bankruptcy and flees the relationship, Charles would then find himself in the empty position of being a creditor without any debtor present to meet his demands. As long as Anita is willing to remain a Deficit Doormat, the balance between her submission and her husband's demanding entitlements creates a dysfunctional symbiosis. But Anita's healthy awakening and her resolve to shed her Doormat role have now forced the relationship to a new plateau. Either Charles must begin to treat his wife as a real, separate person and allow their relationship to mature, or he can stubbornly maintain his role as an Entitleist—on his own.

TYPE 3. EMOTIONAL LOAN SHARKS: OPPORTUNISTIC PREDATORS

In the seedy underworld of cash exchange lurk menacing loan sharks seeking out and taking advantage of those in dire need of money. Loan Sharks prey on the economically wounded, the disadvantaged and the desperate, leveraging them into shackles of debt which carry exorbitant interest rates. If the hapless debtor is unable to cough up the required payments right on time, stringent methods of collection are utilized—a persuasive visit from Guido and Sal, leg-breakers extraordinaire, will usually do the trick. If not, debtors may find themselves in deeper trouble—six feet deep, or perhaps twenty fathoms.

Emotional Loan Sharks are the relational counterparts of these financial pirates. They search out those who are emotionally injured or vulnerable and opportunistically plunge them into ever deepening debt as a means of entrapping them in a web of obligation.

Emotional Loan Sharks are agile
predators who have evolved with an
instinct for opportunistically feeding on
the weaknesses of others.

These shrewd scavengers have the uncanny ability to pick up the scent of those in distress. Like their marine namesakes, Emotional Loan Sharks are drawn to their wounded prey by the smell of blood. They may travel in packs or operate as solitary hunters, but either way, their ability to pursue, manipulate and destroy far exceeds the defensive resources of their feeble targets. Sharks come in a variety of shapes and sizes—some massive and fearsome, others camouflaged to appear like their prey. Victims floundering in emotional distress may not be aware that they are dealing with Loan Sharks until it is too late. Emotional Loan Sharks often appear kind, concerned, generous and helpful, but their agendas are always to exert control and gain something in the long run. They may initially say things like:

- *"Here, let me help you with that."*

- *"It's no problem at all."*

- *"Why don't you use mine?"*

- *"You can always pay me back later."*

However, after they have extended themselves, and created a sense of debt, Emotional Loan Sharks will zero in for the kill. Once they have established themselves as creditors, the tone of their communication changes dramatically:

- *"After all I've done for you."*

- *"The least you owe me is..."*

- *"What kind of thanks is that?"*

- *"Where would you be now if it weren't for me?"*

Once Loan Sharks have mapped out their territories and sunk their teeth into their prey, they never relinquish their position as creditor. They insist on continuous payment and slyly instill feelings of endless obligation. The insatiable Shark will never allow any debt to be fully paid off.

As long as *Emotional Loan Sharks* can preserve their status as Creditor, they can continue to extract payment.

The relationship of Gloria and Jimmy provides a glimpse into the murky world of the Emotional Loan Shark.

Gloria was twenty-eight years old and had been divorced for ten months. She met her current boyfriend, Jimmy, on the rebound during the final stages of her divorce. Jimmy was a co-worker who had always been friendly and attentive. When he first heard that Gloria was having marital difficulties, he offered his emotional support and concern.

Gloria described his initial gestures of friendship. "He told me about his own divorce and was willing to listen to me whenever I needed to talk. In the beginning we would go to lunch together or sometimes meet after work. I would call him some nights just to hear another voice. He seemed like such a nice guy—always there to listen to me, and so understanding.

"As time went by, I felt myself becoming more and more dependent on Jimmy. The divorce really tore me up and I didn't want to burden my friends and family with the messy details or my own depression. Jimmy kept telling me to not bother them and to lean on him. When I look back now I can see how much I withdrew from everyone else and isolated myself with Jimmy.

"The relationship with Jimmy had never been romantic, but it had always been affectionate. Jimmy would hold me when I needed to cry. But one night things changed. I remember being really depressed all day at work and Jimmy took me out for some drinks to try and cheer me up. Well, I got pretty drunk and we ended up back at my apartment in bed together. To be honest, I don't remember much of that night, but after that, the relationship was never the same.

"After we slept together it was like Jimmy felt he owned me or something. I began to see a different side of him that I didn't like at all. From then on, whenever he wanted sex he would remind me of how much he had done for me in the past—how he had stood by me and was the only one who really cared. If I didn't give in to him, he would threaten to leave me. I was so scared of being abandoned again that I would do whatever he wanted. I couldn't stand the thought of being left alone. I felt more and more obligated to keep Jimmy happy and didn't care what it took.

"As time went on, he became more demanding and domineering. The caring, sensitive side of him all but disappeared. It was frightening. He kept telling me I would be nothing without him and I began to believe it was actually true. He said really ugly things—how no other man would ever want me now that I was divorced and would be seen as spoiled goods. My self-esteem kept plunging lower and lower.

"Then one night Jimmy came home and told me he needed two thousand dollars to get himself out of some kind of trouble. When I told him I didn't have the money he got so angry I thought he was going to hit me. After he stormed out, I realized how trapped and scared I was. I knew I couldn't go on with things the way they were. But later, when I tried to talk with Jimmy about how I felt, he just threw it all back in my face—like I was just a selfish person who only knew how to take from others. I guess that's when it hit me—when I knew I had to get out of this relationship no matter how scared I was. I realized this man was slowly sucking all of the life out of me and that he was never going to stop. I packed up my things the next morning after he went to work and moved back in with my parents."

To Gloria's credit, she found the strength to leave this destructive relationship. She realized that Jimmy wasn't ever going to change back into the person he initially had portrayed himself to be. She could see in retrospect that his ingratiating gestures during her time of transition and vulnerability were merely his way of setting the hook and gaining control. As long as he could keep her feeling insecure and indebted to him, Jimmy could preserve his status as creditor and continue to extract whatever payments he wanted. Jimmy, the Emotional Loan Shark, fed on power, sex and control. He had stalked and entrapped his victim patiently and had no intentions of releasing her.

Emotional Loan Sharks are persistent in both their hunting behavior and their ongoing demands for payments. They extort and control their victims through the use of belittlement, accusations, and threats. Fortunately for Gloria, she was able to determine that her only healthy course of action was to unilaterally withdraw from this insidiously damaging relationship. Jimmy tried his best through guilt and harassment to prevent her escape, but Gloria managed to extricate herself and get away. She retreated with some deep emotional scars and fear of Jimmy's ongoing pursuit, but Gloria, in the end, was free. Though not unscathed, she had survived the perilous attack of an Emotional Loan Shark and lived to tell about it.

TYPE 4. GUILT EXTORTIONISTS: MARTYRS WITH AN AGENDA

There is a story that tells of a Jewish mother who gave her son Benjamin two different shirts for his birthday. When Ben came out later from his room wearing one, she looked at him with pain in her voice and sorrow in her eyes and said, "So, what's the matter, you didn't like the other one?"

Guilt is one of the most potent and pervasive motivators in the realm of human experience. It is a universal emotion which ranks with shame, fear and pleasure as primary determinants of human behavior. Because of its prevalence and power, guilt is the tool of choice for many a manipulative creditor.

The American Heritage Dictionary defines "extortion" as the illegal use of one's official position or powers to obtain property, funds or patronage. The word itself is derived from the Latin, *extorquere—ex + torquere*: to twist, to wrench out. The courtroom use of the word in our culture is akin to "blackmail" in which money or something of value is extracted through the threat of disclosing some kind of discrediting information.

Emotional Extortionists are the relational blackmailers of the world. They coerce others to act in whatever ways they desire by skillfully inducing guilt. These manipulative wizards have actually refined the use of guilt to an art form. Guilt Extortionists may initially appear weak and selfless, but their sacrifices and altruistic behavior have heavy-duty emotional strings attached. Their showcased suffering is a tenacious tentacle of control and a set-up for later demands of repayment. Guilt Extortionists may appear as angels of mercy, but there are always webs of self-interest behind their cloaks of sainthood.

Guilt Extortionists have the appearance
of a *Deficit Doormat* but the instinct
and teeth of an *Emotional Loan Shark.*

The utterances of suffering and sacrifice from Guilt Extortionists always have catches:

- *"Oh, don't worry about me, I'll manage somehow."*

- "Here, take mine . . . I can do without."

- "Go ahead, I'm in no hurry . . . Where would I be going anyway?"

- "Oh no, I wouldn't want to impose."

Once an Extortionist succeeds in getting someone to feel guilty, his status and power as creditor become unshakable. From his position as mistreated sufferer, he can manipulate as effectively as the Loan Shark to suck out the most from every ripe situation.

The case of Tim provides a telling example of a Guilt Extortionist in action.

Tim is a thirty-six-year-old electrician who has been out of work for nine weeks following a minor back injury he sustained on the job. He has been receiving worker's compensation and disability and fears he may not be able to return to work for at least a year. Soon after the accident, Tim called his older sister Chelsea and asked if he could move in with her and her husband for a few weeks while he got his feet back on the ground. Chelsea related the story as follows.

"Tim said he couldn't make rent on his disability checks and that his landlord was threatening eviction. We have a spare bedroom in the back and my husband Bob and I decided it would be all right if he stayed with us for a few weeks while he looked for a cheaper apartment. Tim made it sound like he would be out on the street if we didn't help him. He went on and on about how much his back hurt and how insensitive I was being for my reluctance to immediately help him out.

"I guess you can tell I was skeptical from the start. Tim's always been kind of a scammer, but Bob thought we should give my brother the benefit of the doubt. Anyway, three months went by and it started to become apparent that Tim had no intentions of looking for a new apartment. He slept in late on weekdays, stayed out drinking to all hours, but always seemed to be around when dinner was served or his clothes needed washing. He did pay us $100 a month to help with rent, but you should have heard his performance each time he wrote the check. He made us feel like we were stealing his last nickel.

"On weekends, when Bob was around, Tim made sure to get up early and spend time with Bob fixing things up around the house. That part was great because Bob isn't what you would call handy. They fixed some broken windows, re-wired the basement and attic, and even started a redwood deck for the side yard. His back always seemed to be fine whenever he was impressing Bob with his hard work. Bob was ecstatic. I've never seen him so proud. Tim even convinced him to buy some new power tools so that he could teach Bob how to make furniture.

"Well, after about six months of having Tim mooch off us, I reached my threshold and raised the issue that no one else was talking about—when was Tim going to move? You would have thought I had hit Tim in the head with a brick—he went on and on about how bad his back was, how destitute he was having to survive on disability, and how hard he had been trying, despite his injury, to help with things around the house. He sulked and pouted and made us feel like we were the lowest form of slime for even suggesting he move.

"And if that wasn't enough, you should have heard Bob. I couldn't believe it. Without taking me aside to discuss things first, Bob had actually intimated to Tim that he could stay as long as he needed until he found a decent apartment. I was furious. It was like my own husband turned on me. Tim didn't have to say a word; Bob went on to plead his case for him: 'Your brother needs us right now. It's not like he's trying to get a free ride. Look how much he's done around here to try and help us out. The least we owe him is a place to eat and sleep until he's able to work again. He is your brother after all.'

"Finally I sat down with both Bob and Tim to try and hash the situation out. That was my biggest mistake."

Chelsea asked her brother, "Tim, it's been six months that you've been living here. I've reached the point of feeling like you have overstayed your welcome and now you are just taking advantage of the situation. I also resent the way you're trying to kiss up to Bob and play off his sympathy. Don't you think it's about time you showed a little responsibility and started taking some control of your own life?"

Tim angrily responded, "Responsibility! Where do you get off talking about responsibility. Who do you think was home taking care of things after Dad died? It was easy for you. You were already out of the house and off across the country studying music. You had your room and board and tuition checks rolling in from the money Dad had set aside. But after he died, there was no more money. I sure as hell didn't have the luxury of anyone subsidizing my dreams. I had to work for a living while I tried my best to keep Mom from drinking herself to death. And you have the nerve to accuse me of being irresponsible!"

Chelsea defended herself, "That's not fair, Tim. It's not my fault Dad got sick. What was I supposed to do, drop out of school and come back home?"

"Hey, you made your choices and did what you wanted," Tim told her. "I never even had a chance to think about options. And now, you have Bob's cush income to take care of you in this beautiful house while you still get to do whatever it is you damned well please. Well, some of us haven't had things quite as easy. Some of us don't get everything handed to them on a silver platter. And now, for the first time in my life when I've really had to ask anyone in my family for help, you act like I'm some kind of low-life scrounger. Are you really so caught up in your selfishness that you can't even help out your own brother? Why don't you climb down off your high horse long enough to see how the rest of the world lives."

Not all Guilt Extortionists are as extreme as Tim, but the underlying dynamic is always similar. These expert manipulators create debt by making others feel guilt-ridden and obligated. Because their power emanates from their creditor status, Extortionists have no desire to let go of their claim to compensation. Rather, the goal of the Extortionist is to insure that debts are never fully liquidated so that they can perpetuate indebtedness and continue to elicit payments and benefits.

Tim's goal is to maintain a low cost residence with his sister and keep his disability income flowing as long as he can. Because he knows the limits of his credibility with his sister, Tim initially targets Bob as a point of leverage. Bob is not around on weekdays to witness Tim's free-loading style. Instead, Bob experiences his brother-in-law as incapacitated yet industrious. Tim succeeds in lulling Bob into a state of appreciation not only for the projects Tim has orchestrated, but also for helping Bob find new confidence in his own abilities to work with his hands. Bob's gratitude translates into a sense of indebtedness which is just the hook Tim needs to carry out his extortion.

However, Chelsea, in her own experience and wisdom, sees through the ruse and refuses to accept the fabricated debt. She attempts to bring the real issues to the surface by an open discussion, but Tim responds by letting her have it with both barrels. At this point, Tim kicks into high gear as a master Guilt Extortionist. He pulls out his heavy artillery and assaults his sister with a barrage of blame for all of the privileges she has enjoyed and all of the hardships he has had to endure. He strategically finds her weakest point and plunges in his bayonet of guilt. Chelsea tries to resist the blade, but Tim twists it relentlessly to secure his status as creditor. The question then becomes whether Chelsea will yield to his strategic extortion or whether she will be able to resist her own guilt in order to put an end to the current stronghold of Tim's manipulation and entrenchment.

TYPE 5. BEAN COUNTERS: TIT-FOR-TAT BARGAINERS

In the world of business, there are legions of skilled professionals whose sole jobs are tallying the financial scores. These meticulous, analytic numericists come with a wide variety of titles—bookkeepers, planners, auditors, analysts, CFOs, CPAs, tax consultants and financial advisors. But regardless of their education, name plates or credentials, each utilizes a spectrum of tools ranging from mechanical pencils to computer programs in their quest to accurately account for every penny earned and spent. These exacting accountants are commonly referred to as the "Bean Counters" of the business world. And despite our tendency to poke fun at them, in the world of commerce, they are indispensable since their final summation of the bottom line heralds the ultimate success or failure of any enterprise.

In the world of human relationships, however, success is never determined by a precise tally of debits and credits. When it comes to emotional intimacy, relational Bean Counters accomplish little apart from frustrating and tormenting their partners. Relational Bean

Counters are niggling, scorekeeping negotiators who expect to receive something in return for even the slightest favor. Their anthem is: *quid pro quo*—I'll give to you, but you must equally give back to me. Each proffered kindness becomes a claim for something later.

Bean Counters **never give freely—**
there is always a hook.
They are Givers with an Attitude.

Bean Counters' unquenchable demands for reciprocity create an atmosphere laden by discomfort and saturated with suspicion. Because they live with one eye fixed on the balance sheet, their mates constantly shiver under the cold shadow of scrutiny and micro-measurement. After enduring relationships with tit-for-tat Bean Counters for any length of time, their partners become anxious over every positive gesture extended, asking themselves:

- *"What cost will there be?"*

- *"What strings are attached?"*

- *"Do I dare accept what's offered?"*

The nervous recipients have been sensitized to wonder what price will ultimately be extracted to balance the equation in the mind of their bean counting partner. The net effect of this balance sheet mentality is that even the most generous mates are insidiously drawn into hyper-awareness of the potential weight of every emotional bean. Out of sheer self-protection, the naturally magnanimous partners are forced to mimic the exacting style of their calculating cohorts.

Relational Bean Counters can be identified by phrases such as:

- *"It's your turn, I did it last time."*

- *"I thought we agreed to have an egalitarian relationship."*

- *"I don't mean to be petty, but . . ."*

- *"Well, I did it for you, so I figured you would do the same for me."*

The underlying motive for Bean Counters extending themselves in the first place is to set the stage for laying claim to some form of future compensation. They give now to get what they want later. They use every act of giving on their part as the creation of a new debt. Some Bean Counters are fair-minded and see relationships as a two-way street—feeling that their partners also deserve equal payment for any favor extended. But other Bean Counters are narcissistically skewed to their own advantage—demanding payment for every debt owed to them, but expecting others to give freely without any strings attached. Either way, relationships with Bean Counters become suffused with tension and confinement. There is never any room for spontaneous giving or unencumbered love. Stanley and Joy's relationship serves as a good illustration of this phenomenon.

Stanley and Joy have been living together for eight months. Joy is thirty-four and works as a marketing manager. Stanley is a thirty-seven-year-old systems analyst for a software firm. Joy began to have growing discontentment with what started out as a promising relationship.

"Stanley has this quirk about everything being fair," she explained. "It's like an obsession with him. I'm all for equal rights and shared responsibility, but I hate feeling like we're always keeping score. He actually keeps lists and charts to track chores and expenses.

"At first I liked the idea of alternating cooking nights, splitting the rent and maintaining separate accounts. But after a while things got out of hand. Now we're down to a level of whose parents received the most expensive gift and whose turn it is to tip the paperboy. It's driving me nuts. I feel like he thinks I'm trying to cheat him at every turn. Stanley doesn't see any problem—but, of course, I'm the one under the microscope."

Stanley was defensive of his position and did not feel he was being overbearing or unreasonable.

He stated his rationale clearly and succinctly. "I've been in lopsided relationships before and I refuse to be taken advantage of again. I love Joy. I'm not a selfish person and I'm willing to give a lot, but I just want to be sure that we keep things on an even playing field. I really don't see what the big issue is. What's wrong with fairness and precision? It seems to me that the best way to insure equality is to keep a careful account of things. Otherwise you're just guessing."

At this point in the session, Stanley glanced at his watch:

"I hope I haven't used up more than my share of time. Go ahead, Joy, it's your turn to talk again."

Joy rolled her eyes in exasperation, "See what I mean, Doctor."

Stanley's *quid-pro-quo* methodology has proven far too extreme for Joy. While he may view himself as reasonable and fair, Joy has come to see him as petty and distrustful. Stanley has obviously been burned before in previous relationships and Joy appears to have inherited some residual debt from these past inequities. Stanley's position as creditor grows out of his old resentments as well as his current, sterile insistence on relational scorekeeping. Both problems—past and present—need to be addressed if Stanley and Joy are to preserve their love relationship.

It is important to understand that it is not only the overt behavior of Bean Counters that creates relational rifts, but it is also the underlying messages conveyed by insistence on exact accounting. By tracking all exchanges and demanding fastidious balances, Bean Counters communicate an abject lack of faith. The inescapable implication is that their partners cannot be relied on or trusted. In our example, Stanley might believe he is genuinely acting to protect Joy's best interest, but his method and manner in the end serve only to alienate Joy and leave her feeling demeaned and demoralized. Stanley may think he is preserving fairness and balance, but he risks losing his relationship if he persists in his *quid-pro-quo* approach. Scorekeeper Stanley needs to factor in the cost of his bean counting before he finds himself tallying up a new balance sheet with only one column—his!

CONCLUSION

We have looked at five distinct types of creditors—all extreme examples of individuals who operate at the far end of the emotional spectrum. The fact is that all of us have a bit of Mark, Entitleist, Loan Shark, Guilt Extortionist and Bean Counter in us. None of us is exempt from these detrimental behavior patterns, and so it is vital for us to pay close attention to our own creditor conduct and the impact it has on others. Observation of these tendencies can be an invaluable avenue of insight into our own contribution to relational problems when creditor behavior disrupts free-flowing intimacy.

Through the last two chapters, we have examined portraits of various debtor and creditor types. While descriptive labels can prove useful tools, the goal here is not to pigeonhole people into tight diagnostic boxes. Instead, identifying generic patterns of behavior and interaction provides a common vocabulary for discussion and understanding. Diagnostic classifications should be viewed as maps—they can present important information that allows us to understand many things about the terrain. But we must never mistake the map for the actual landscape. Maps are merely pieces of paper with symbolic markings—the real landscape is a living entity, infinitely more complex than any two-dimensional sheet of paper which depicts it. As we reflect on types of relationship debtors and creditors, it is essential to remember that these categories are only descriptive chartings. Ultimately, we are talking about real human beings who will always transcend any labels we affix.

Chapter 5

DEBTOR OR CREDITOR? HOW DO I KNOW?
The Signpoints of Recognition

A Promise made is a debt unpaid,
and the trail has its own stern code.
　　　　　　　　　　　　　- Robert W. Service

The vast majority of relational debts lie beneath conscious awareness. These debts are like undetected diseases which manifest themselves as external outbreaks. The distress may erupt in a variety of
relational symptoms: withdrawal, pouting, criticism, bickering, sarcasm or rage. However, regardless of what form the upheaval may
take, the surface behavior is always indicative of a more fundamental problem—the underlying emotional debt.

In medical treatment, the alleviation of painful physical symptoms is an important focus, but for a genuine cure, it is essential to
trace external indicators all the way down to the root disease. The
same principle holds true for relationships. Counseling partners to
stop fighting, display affection, listen attentively or express their
needs can all help in diminishing surface tension; but if a core debt is
left to fester, that debt will continue to infect the relationship and will
eventually manifest again as new symptoms.

**Emotional debts cannot be resolved by
treating surface symptoms any more
than leprosy can be cured with skin cream.**

81

The external symptoms of relational stress, however, are key signposts deserving our close attention—they are always the indelible signature of a submerged debt. Just as a high fever provides evidence of an internal infection, the symptomatic behavior patterns of creditors and debtors trace a direct pathway to unresolved emotional debt. The challenge to any troubled relationship thus becomes one of properly identifying creditors and debtors as a means of pinpointing, rooting out and eradicating malignant debts.

Surprisingly, the categorization of debtors and creditors is not always self-evident. One or both partners may have no immediate awareness of either a debt's existence or their own personal role as creditor or debtor. Fortunately, awareness can be brought to the forefront—there are emotional signposts which unerringly distinguish which role an individual is playing out.

While the wide spectrum of human emotions might seem too complex and unwieldy to systematize, there are in fact two distinct families of emotions which encompass the gamut. The two overriding emotions which circumscribe all others are GUILT and RESENTMENT. I have found in the process of treating hundreds of couples that these two emotions are key to the discovery and proper identification of debtors and creditors. The generic experience of Guilt is the underlying feeling which consistently characterizes all debtors; while a dominant emotion of Resentment inevitably points to a creditor.

All relational distress signals are subspecies of these two families of human emotion. The continuum of specific feelings subsumed under the umbrella emotions of Guilt and Resentment reflect various degrees and expressions of each:

RESENTMENT	GUILT
irritation	twinge of responsibility
annoyance	inadequacy
aggravation	regret
anger	remorse
contempt	embarrassment
rage	shame
hatred	self-loathing
vengefulness	self-recrimination

A couple's turmoil might be expressed, for example, through one partner's active contempt or the other's passive remorse—but the problems will be traceable to either a pervasive feeling of guilt or an agitated sense of resentment. The governing emotion may be unacknowledged or disguised, but a persistent search will lead to one of the two dominant feelings.

GUILT

Guilt is the emblem of all debtors. It is the definitive indicator of those who feel that they owe. The case of Bill and Julia provides a clear illustration of debtor's guilt.

Bill and Julia sought counseling because Julia felt their relationship drifting apart. She had tried to confront Bill many times on her own, but was frustrated by his deflections.

Julia described their situation. "For the last few months Bill has been so sullen and detached. He's completely withdrawn and hardly says more than 'good morning' and 'good night'. He still interacts with the kids, but for some reason he's pulled away from me. I can't tell if he's depressed or angry or what. I just know that I'm tired of feeling like I've done something wrong. I want to know why he's treating me this way and when its going to stop."

Initially, Bill tried to deny the level of his detachment and pointed to business pressures and work stress as the reason behind his moodiness. He offered weak apologies and superficial excuses which did not seem to account for the level of his depressed state or his emotional withdrawal from Julia. Finally, after several futile sessions of Bill talking around issues, a strong focus was put on the aura of guilt which Bill seemed to radiate. When questions about his guilt were raised, a deep chord was struck and Bill finally opened up and disclosed the real source of his despondency.

"Five months ago I invested our retirement account in a start-up company. I tried to talk it over with you, Julia, if you remember and you said you were against it. You thought it was too risky to stake our future on. Well, I went ahead anyway. I was personal friends with the company's president and I was absolutely convinced it was a sure thing. Well, it wasn't . . . we've already lost over half our money and the stock is still dropping. Over seventy-thousand dollars is down the drain—our hopes for a secure future . . . I haven't had the nerve to tell you the truth. I keep hoping the stock will turn around, but it's been a continual decline. If I sell now, we're going to take a horrible beating. I guess I've been hoping against hope and praying that the stock will go back up so that I could retrieve our losses and never have to ever tell you about the whole mess I created. I feel so stupid for what I've done and so horrible for acting behind your back. I don't think I've ever done anything worse in my whole life."

Bill's guilt is clearly the central emotion steering the relationship down a dangerous path of isolation and confusion. Because Julia had no knowledge of the precipitating event (Bill's financial debacle) or any comprehension of Bill's guilt, his surface behavior of withdrawal remained an irritating mystery to her. Bill's depression and disengagement are direct expressions of his guilt, which itself is the definitive sign that he is operating as a debtor. In Bill's case, it is easy to trace a path to the origin of the emotional debt—his investment decision contrary to Julia's wishes and the ongoing disastrous loss of their retirement savings.

Guilt is always the distinguishing
hallmark of an emotional debtor.

Once Bill's atypical behavior is seen as stemming from guilt, then there is a logical linkage to his position as debtor. With this connection, the debt itself surfaces and the marital problem can finally come to light. Bill, the debtor, feels that he owes enormous recompense to Julia, the unaware creditor, as a result of his poor judgment and betrayal of her trust. Now that Julia is fully apprised of the debt, she can assume her rightful position as creditor and only then can real options for resolution be explored. The final settlement may be complex and difficult, but clarification of the roles of debtor and creditor paves the way for relational energy to be directed in a positive path towards reconciliation.

RESENTMENT

While guilt always marks the existence of a relationship debtor, resentment inevitably reveals the presence of a relationship creditor.

The resentment may be expressed through many diverse patterns of behavior: active hostility, biting humor, sexual retreat, explosive tirades, internalized depression. Nevertheless, whatever form resentment takes, it is always evidence of an unpaid creditor and a clear indication of a lingering debt. The story of Ray and Sylvia shows a resentful creditor in action.

Ray and Sylvia have been married six years and have experienced their share of ups and downs. They had been through therapy twice before and had appeared to have resolved past conflicts. However, once again they seemed to have reached an emotional impasse. This time Ray initiated getting help because of Sylvia's recent outbursts.

Ray voiced his concerns. "I've never seen her like this before. It's getting worse each day. It doesn't matter whether I try to act nice or stand up to her, she just keeps being unreasonable and bitchy. I don't know if I've done something to make her mad or whether her hormones are out of whack, but I'm tired of putting up with it."

When Sylvia was questioned about her behavior she admitted to her hostility, but initially was unable to pinpoint where her anger was coming from. "I just find myself getting more and more irritated with Ray. The minute he enters the room I tense up. Any little thing he does seems to set me off."

Ray and Sylvia agreed that it might help for Sylvia to have an individual session solely for the purpose of exploring the roots of her hair-trigger anger. By the time Sylvia arrived for this session, she had already made a connection between her current aggravation and a series of events that occurred about three months earlier.

Sylvia explained her resentment. "I didn't realize it at the time, but I'm really angry about the whole week Ray's brother came out to visit us last April. I knew that the two of them had planned to go fishing for three days, but I really expected that the rest of the visit we would all do things together. The way it turned out, they had a great time playing golf, going to a ball game, staying up to all hours, while I was left home alone. Ray had taken the week off, but I still had to get up and go into work each morning. Even with my work schedule, I cooked and cleaned-up after them during Ray's brother's whole vacation. I wanted Ray to have a good time with his brother, but I expected to be more than just their maid."

Sylvia became clear about her hurt and anger and agreed to bring this up with Ray in their next session. Ray seemed quite surprised by Sylvia's description of her upset about the week of his brother's visit.

Ray had experienced their time together very differently. As he explained, "I never knew you were feeling that way while Tom was here. It didn't occur to me you might have wanted to spend time with us while we did a bunch of 'guy things'. If we had known you were feeling left out we would have planned things a lot differently. I never meant to hurt you. I thought you were going out of your way to avoid us. "

"I was, Ray, but that was only because I thought you two didn't want me to ruin your fun. You both acted like I didn't exist. I felt like you two at least owed me some appreciation for everything I did."

"I'm sorry, Sylvia. I wish you would have said something before."

Sylvia's recent anger is a manifestation of her resentment over being ignored and unappreciated. In the current instance, her resentment signifies Sylvia's role as creditor—feeling that Ray owes her compensation for the hospitality she extended to his brother as well as punitive damages for their thoughtless neglect.

Resentment, **regardless of how it is expressed, is the defining benchmark of any relationship creditor.**

Sylvia's resentment provides the necessary clue that a debt exists. Once her role as creditor is unveiled, the disruptive debt can be discovered and Ray, the previously unaware debtor, can direct his own energy towards some kind of suitable settlement. The specific debt resolution might take many forms (we will explore the spectrum of debt settlements in our next chapter), but the ability to reconcile the debt can only occur after there is a clear identification of the creditor and the debtor.

A FOUR STEP PROCESS FOR DEBT DISCOVERY

The encompassing categories of GUILT or RESENTMENT serve as powerful assessment tools for recognizing the presence of debtors and creditors. Once a debtor or creditor is identified, then a gateway to the hidden debt is opened. The initial challenge, therefore, is making the determination of whether guilt or resentment is the predominant emotion governing relational distress. Distinguishing guilt from resentment might seem easy or obvious on the surface, but emotional identification is not always self-evident.

For many individuals it is extremely difficult and even baffling to recognize and label their own feelings. Some people have a disruptive breach between their emotions and their emotional awareness. It is not that these individuals are devoid of feelings, but rather that they are somehow dissociated from their own emotional experiences. Their situation is analogous to an anesthetized dental patient (injected locally with Novocain) who is impervious to the pain of the drill. The stimulus of the drill is present, but the experience of the drilling is removed. For the emotionally detached person, external events will register at some deep level, but the emotion (anger, sadness, hurt, joy) will not be cognitively detected or spontaneously felt. This detachment can be so severe in some people that the very idea having and expressing emotions can seem totally foreign.

**Emotionally disconnected individuals
do not spontaneously feel their feelings.**

When confronted about their feelings, the emotionally detached person will usually respond with statements such as:

- *"What makes you think I'm angry?"*

- *"What do you mean I must be upset; you're the one ranting and raving."*

- *"I don't think I'm depressed."*

- *"I'm not sure I know what you mean—I don't feel anything."*

There are a number of explanations as to why people become separated from their own emotionality. The cause for this puzzling chasm may be found in physical and neurological dysfunctions, social conditioning or the development of specific psychological defense mechanisms. The gap between emotion and awareness could be reflective of anything from a brain lesion to an oppressively strict childhood where emotional expression was shunned or punished.

A frequent cause of psychological dissociation is intense trauma which forces a break between experience and awareness, thus allowing the victim to survive the specific ordeal (assault, rape, torture, natural disaster) without having to truly feel the horror. People who cope in this manner often dispassionately describe their wrenching experiences as though they happened to someone else. Such exaggerated emotional distancing is an extreme example of the kind of emotional detachment all of us experience to some degree. For all of us, a large portion of our psychological experience is deflected to our unconscious, a fact which gives ample testimony to the universal phenomena of emotional dissociation.

However, when we are detached from our own feelings, we ultimately find ourselves detached from the people around us. Healthy relationships require that we connect with our partners and express ourselves at emotional levels that are congruent with our experiences. We must know what we feel and be willing to voice our emotions openly.

Emotional self-awareness is always a prerequisite for meaningful self-expression and intimacy.

Whenever people are confused about the nature of their feelings, emotional awareness can be accessed through careful examinations of their behavior and their interactions. People's conduct and reactions are the clearest avenue to their emotions. The four-step process which follows provides a systematic tool for recognizing surface behaviors and categorizing underlying emotions. Once core emotions are identified, creditors and debtors can be designated and the existing debts can be spotlighted and addressed.

STEP 1. IDENTIFYING PROBLEM BEHAVIORS:
How Am I Acting?
Most couple therapy sessions begin with one person describing disturbing changes in how his or her partner has been *acting*. The first clue that something is awry in a relationship is usually atypical or problematic behavior.

- *"She's been so cold and distant."*

- *"Everything he says lately is sarcastic and biting."*

- *"I've never seen him so angry. He actually punched his fist right through the wall."*

- *"She started sleeping in the guest room."*

- *"Now he is drinking heavily almost every night."*

There are times when all of us act without any awareness of what we are doing. We can be so wrapped up in outside distractions that we often become oblivious to our immediate actions and the attitudes we convey to others. Like a parade of lemmings, we march unconsciously through our daily routines, paying scant attention to our own behavior or its effects. Because of our propensity for self-absorption and preoccupation, the first step to any relational change must involve mindful attentiveness and acknowledgment of our actions and their impact.

In the following example of Carol and Tom, it is Carol's direct feedback which leads to Tom's recognition of his problem behavior.

"Why have you been so irritable and critical lately?" Carol asked. "Every time I've tried to talk to you this past week, you've snapped at me. What are you so upset about?"

Tom answered defensively, "Nothing's the matter. I think you're just being overly sensitive."

Carol didn't accept Tom's response. "I don't think so. Last night you came home and jumped all over me about the living room being a mess. Since when have you ever cared about things being messy? This morning you yelled at me about running out of cat food. Come on, Tom, something's bugging you. What is it?"

Tom, realizing Carol was right, apologized. "I didn't mean to jump on you. I guess I have been kind of edgy. I'm sorry."

"That's putting it mildly," Carol remarked. "Come on, I'd like to know what you're upset about."

Tom had been unaware that he was acting differently until Carol pointed out exactly what she had been observing and experiencing. At first, his reaction to her feedback was flat denial, but Tom was willing to listen openly long enough to consider the validity of Carol's perceptions. Whether from outside observation or through self-reflection, it is always vital to bring to conscious awareness a realistic assessment of our behavior patterns and their effect on others. Once the behaviors are identified, exploration into the causes which govern these external actions can follow.

**Surface behaviors are always the
visible signs of underlying emotions.**

STEP 2. IDENTIFYING EMOTIONS:
What submerged feelings are portrayed by my behavior?

After troubling behavior has been defined and acknowledged, the nature of the impelling emotion can be pursued. Sometimes particular behaviors portray specific emotions: throwing a plate clearly indicates anger, while apologizing profusely signifies remorse or guilt. In many instances, surface behaviors provide only a vague or distorted picture of the actual motivating feeling: silence may be indicative of anger, depression, or merely fatigue; sarcastic teasing could reflect a gamut of emotions ranging from playful affection to camouflaged hostility. The real motivation behind any behavior pattern may or may not be immediately apparent to the person displaying the pattern.

For instance, we may believe at first that we are only "teasing" our partner in an endearing manner, but self-reflection or our mate's upset may yield a deeper truth that, indeed, there is a covert message of resentment behind our veil of humor. In a similar vein, we initially might interpret our passive silence to be a result of weariness, when, in actuality, if we are pressed to look behind our uncommunicative withdrawal, there may be threads of fear or guilt.

Establishing these connections between surface behaviors and underlying feelings thus requires a certain courage to look beyond immediate impressions and confront our true motives. Grasping the heart of our emotions demands relentless self-questioning which will ultimately produce an unmistakable resonance—that "gut feeling" of really knowing. This process of searching for self-truth can prove the most challenging part of any process of transformation, especially when the feelings involved are intense and deep-seated. Courageously facing the unvarnished reality of our raw emotions and directly owning up to them in the presence of our partners are both arduous and noble endeavors. The truth can be embarrassing, humiliating or even terrifying, but ultimately, persevering through the ordeal of disclosure gives rise to a cathartic sense of clarity, integrity and alignment. When we are willing to fight against the natural human tendencies toward rationalization, defensiveness and righteous justification, only then are we able to directly confront our true emotions and label them for what they are.

STEP 3. CREDITOR OR DEBTOR:
Do I feel RESENTMENT or GUILT?
When we have faced our personal truths and identified our underlying emotions accurately, we can then characterize our dominant feeling as indicative of either Resentment or Guilt. Only then can we address the underlying cause of those feelings.

Emotions falling under the category of Resentment are characterized by elements of aggressive blame, irritability or hostility. The family of emotions under the heading of Guilt is earmarked by avoidance, shameful withdrawal and dread.

GUILT implodes; *RESENTMENT* explodes.

After tracing the emotion we really feel to either Guilt or Resentment, we can figure out whether the role of creditor or debtor follows from our own definition—feeling Resentment denotes we are emotional creditors while feeling Guilt points to debtors.

STEP 4. FINDING THE SOURCE OF DEBT:
What happened to make me a debtor or creditor?
Determining the existence of a debtor or creditor points the way toward debts that have remained submerged from our awareness. Once we have discovered that we are a debtor or creditor, we begin to ask questions such as:

- *"What happened to make me feel so resentful?"*

- *"When did this sense of guilt take hold?"*

- *"What circumstances led me to feel that something is owed to me?"*

- *"What incident caused me to respond like I need to pay something back?"*

Such definitive questions naturally trace a direct path to the *source* of the emotional debt we are experiencing. By asking ourselves the right question, the precipitating events of debt creation rise up spontaneously into conscious awareness:

- *"I still feel guilty about my affair with Susan two years ago."*

- *"I resent my father for not paying for college."*

- *"I feel horrible for lying to Judy about my gambling debts."*

- *"I'm upset over you're unwillingness to even consider having children."*

- *"I can't get over feeling guilty about the divorce."*

The source of debt may seem petty or may involve a matter of dire import. It may stem from a singular incident or an accumulation of events. It may be a favor extended just a minute ago or a wound which is decades old. The magnitude of the circumstance which caused the debt will often not correlate with the intensity of the emotion manifested. An individual's response may seem way out of proportion to the actual incident, being either dramatically over-inflated or unduly blunted. But regardless of the intensity or duration of the precipitating event, or the level of emotional reaction, acknowledgment of the debt is paramount. Only when the debt source is finally uncovered and defined can the liberating experience of debt resolution become a real possibility.

To summarize, the four progressive steps for identifying relationship debtors, relationship creditors and the origins of emotional debt are:

1. IDENTIFY SURFACE BEHAVIORS
2. CATEGORIZE UNDERLYING EMOTIONS
3. DETERMINE CREDITOR OR DEBTOR STATUS
4. LOCATE ORIGIN OF DEBT

A few examples will illustrate this progression of discovery.

> Jan has been withdrawing from her husband Tim for the past few weeks. She has been quiet and moody. Tim asked her why she has been so distant, but Jan dismissed him by saying, "I'm just tired."
>
> Tim pushed harder for a response. "Come on, Jan, you've been acting like I don't exist. I've never seen you so preoccupied and cut-off (surface behavior). Please tell me what's going on."
>
> "If you want to know the truth, Tim, I've been really depressed and upset with you (underlying emotion)."
>
> "Why? What did I do?" Tim asked.
>
> "I've been angry (Anger = Resentment = Creditor) ever since you told your parents that we would visit them this summer," said Jan. "You told them we would come without ever discussing it with me first (origin of debt)."
>
> "I didn't think it would be such a big deal," he stated.
>
> "Well, it is," said Jan.

Jan's withdrawal from Tim (surface behavior) is a function of her anger (underlying emotion). Since anger clearly falls under the umbrella of Resentment, Jan is functioning in the role of creditor (Resentment = Creditor). Jan's resentment points to the unresolved debt centering on Tim's unilateral decision for them to visit his parents.

The example of Sam shows the identification process at work for a debtor.

> Sam realized he has been avoiding his supervisor for the past week (surface behavior). When he reflected on his discomfort, he realized that he has been feeling uneasy and fearful (Fear = Guilt = Debtor) that his supervisor would confront him about a major shipping error he made that cost the company a significant account (origin of debt).

Sam comes to the awareness of both his debtor status and the origin of this debt through his own process of self-reflection. In his case, there is no other person pointing out the nature and impact of his behavior. Sam is able to use his own discomfort (fear and avoidance = guilt) as a gauge to detect his position as a debtor. This in turn leads to his recognition of the precipitating event (his shipping error) which created the debt.

> **Tracing the linkage of behavior to emotion**
> **and finally to the source of debt is the**
> **essential prerequisite to debt resolution.**

It is often painstaking to follow the step-by-step path from behavior to emotions, from emotions to debtor/creditor status, and finally from debtor/creditor status to debt origin, but the process is helpful, and at times proves indispensable. Clearly, intimate relationships are fraught with emotions which at times are painful and so many couples ignore or deny difficulties. However, the four-step process can overcome this proclivity for sticking our emotional heads in the sand.

Because dealing with difficulties in our intimate relationships can be so difficult, unfortunately, we also have the uncanny tendency of jumping to quick solutions long before the problems are ever fully defined. The challenge to our inherent impatience often becomes one of slowing down our problem-solving efforts long enough to first delineate the full scope of the problem. Otherwise, a barrage of solutions may be fired off in all directions without any clarity about where the target lies. It is a hopelessly flawed strategy: **"Ready . . . Fire . . . Aim."** This well-intentioned yet misguided tactic is a constant cause of new problems rather than a solution to existing ones.

For example, if I assume that my wife is angry at me for failing to buy her the "right" Christmas gift, I might go out the next day and get her a new car. However, if her upset is really over finances, then my solution only serves to compound the problem and intensify her distress. Ready . . . Fire . . . Aim! We prematurely leap to self-defeating solutions in our relationships like this all the time, and it does nothing except get us into more trouble and deeper emotional debt.

Our genuine desire to expedite problem-solving as a way of easing immediate discomfort is certainly understandable. Nevertheless, diving head-first into a pool makes no sense if, once in mid-flight, we realize that the pool is empty. What does make sense—though it often goes against the grain of our desire for instant remedy—is to survey situations carefully before any corrective energy is expended. We need to take the necessary time to scrutinize, evaluate and define problems accurately so that our interventions do hit the mark.

CONCLUSION

It is vital to carefully trace the origins of our emotional debts. The first step involves identifying changes in our outward behaviors. Significant changes in how we are acting are indicators of the feelings which precipitate such change. Although experiencing and categorizing our own feelings can be a difficult task, it is a prerequisite to our personal growth and connection to others.

Once specific emotional states have been determined, these feelings can be categorized under the umbrella emotions of either guilt or resentment. Guilt always characterizes debtors while resentment signifies creditors. The final step is to identify the events which were the root cause of the guilt or resentment. Once the events have been pinpointed, the debt itself is unearthed; only then should the path toward resolution begin. The value of our four-step process is that it forces a systematic slow-down in problem identification which serves to hold us on track. Once our real relationship problems are in focus, we can first take careful aim and then hit the mark.

Chapter 6

DEBT RESOLUTION
Proven Methods for
Settling Emotional Debts

It's a silly game where nobody wins.
                                                    -Thomas Fuller

In the last chapter, we developed a process for the systematic identification of existing emotional debts. Each of us has the power to unearth and define debts which may be blocking our sense of vitality and movement, both as individuals and partners, in relationships. The elevation of hidden debts to a level of conscious awareness is always the first step towards resolution.

But when the time comes for couples to take the crucial steps toward settling emotional debts, *unilateral* awareness is not sufficient in and of itself. It is a vital requisite that *both* parties recognize the *existence* of the debt, even if there is no concurrence that the debt is legitimate or justifiable. This necessary bridge of consensus can be the most challenging prelude to debt settlement, often requiring one partner to suspend his own entrenched version of reality long enough to give credence to an entirely different perspective.

To begin achieving some mutual accord and enriching rather than decreasing the quality of relationship, it is imperative to understand the distinction between *agreeing* that a debt exists and *validating* the debt's legitimacy. If I feel that you owe me something, you may find my conclusion to be outlandish or unjustifiable. So be it, but we are not going to get very far in resolving our impasse until you are able to at least recognize that I truly harbor the feeling of being owed. You may disagree, but your acknowledgment of my feelings is mandatory.

> *All* parties in a debt dynamic must
> acknowledge the debt before
> any settlement is possible.

For most relationships, the formidable stumbling block to mutual acknowledgment is the frustrating fact that one individual's perception can be wildly different from his partner's point of view. One of the undeniable truths about human beings is the limitless diversity of our viewpoints, interpretations and conclusions about the world. One person's supremely rational discernment and arrangement of the data is another person's bizarre and insupportable misperception.

Unfortunately, many of us operate from basic mind-sets that we are unerring observers of objective reality. We are unshakable in our certainty that what we see is indeed what has happened, that what we hear is exactly what has been said. We will go to our graves arguing that we are right about our interpretation of events. To hear some of us in the heat of disagreement would lead to the conclusion that we are endowed with photographic memories, the acuity of eagles, the flawless objectivity of video cassettes, and the intuition of infallible psychics. The truth is that none of us possesses the perfect powers of perception that we sometimes assert. In fact, the illusion of "perfect" perception which we so dogmatically uphold, often turns out to be the very instrument of our relational demise.

THE LIMITATIONS OF HUMAN PERCEPTION

After thousands of therapy hours with clients, I have concluded that if I am to help people in their relationships, my most pressing task is to convince them of the limitations of all perceptual experiences. Until the ever-present fallibilities of our sensors and receptors are accepted, we will remain shackled to our deluded sense of always being right.

It is wholly inadequate to merely describe the flaws of human perception—people will simply not accept the intellectual argument that their observations and recall are often inaccurate. Exercises like the ones which follow provide more powerful demonstrations.

EXERCISE 1. Memorize the following three phrases:

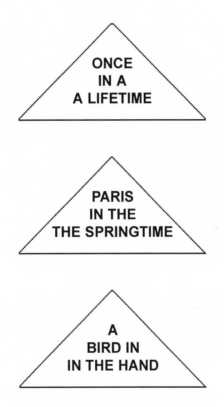

ONCE
IN A
A LIFETIME

PARIS
IN THE
THE SPRINGTIME

A
BIRD IN
IN THE HAND

Keep these phrases in mind and go to the next exercise.

EXERCISE 2. Answer the following questions:

1. The opposite of bottom is __ __ __.
2. You wax a floor with a __ __ __.
3. You use an ax to __ __ __ __.
4. When you come to a green light you __ __ __ __.

EXERCISE 3. While reading the following sentence, count the number of F's and keep that number in your head.

THE FIRST AND FOREMOST RULE OF HUMAN PERCEPTION THAT EACH OF US MUST EMBRACE IS THAT OUR CAPACITY FOR EXPERIENCING REALITY IS ALWAYS FILTERED THROUGH OUR FALLIBLE SENSES, WHICH MOST OF US FEEL ARE INFINITELY ACCURATE.

The three preceding tasks are not high level perceptual challenges, but they will hopefully serve to prove a point. Perhaps what we think we see is not what is actually there. Just possibly, our perfect perception and our objective conclusions are neither perfect nor objective. If reality were truly so static and definable, why is it so that nine out of ten arguments are ultimately over what is real. How often have we heard (or even said) heated rejoinders like:

- *"I never said that!"*

- *"I distinctly remember seeing you do it."*

- *"I heard it with my own ears."*

- *"I know exactly what you meant."*

People argue about who is right and who is wrong, who did what, who said what and what it all meant. The presumption is always, "My perception of what happened is absolutely accurate, while your interpretation is somehow distorted." Each of us has unshakable faith in our sense of objectivity and we will vehemently defend our claim to unerring discernment whenever challenged.

However, experts in human perception start out with a different set of assumptions. Trained police investigators, for instance, know that if they take five different accounts of an auto accident from five different eyewitnesses, each story will vary, and some quite dramatically. The reality of the accident will be filtered through each witness's perception, and the resulting narrative will be skewed by each individual's prejudices, selective memory and personal life experiences.

The childhood game of "Telephone," where a secret is whispered from one person to the next around a circle, is another example of this same phenomenon: by the time the message reaches the last person, it almost certainly will have become radically altered. The original message is progressively warped by the reception and transmission of each player. What starts out as, "You're the best friend I've ever had here" could ultimately transmogrify into something like, "You're a breast fiend and I've had it up to here with you."

As human beings we tend to see and hear what we want and expect rather than what actually exists. Let's go back to the three previous exercises. In **EXERCISE** 1, most people will report seeing "Once in a Lifetime," "Paris in the Springtime" and "A Bird in the Hand." The fact is, people who report "seeing" the phrases this way are exactly right—that is what they *see*, but that is not what is written on the page. The reality of what is on the page is different—each phrase contains a word that is repeated (a a, the the, in in). Our perception tends to filter out the extraneous word to preserve each phrase in a form with which we are familiar. We are apt to see what we want to see or what our minds expect rather than what is actually printed on the page in black and white.

In **EXERCISE** 2, the correct answers are 1) TOP, 2) MOP, 3) CHOP and 4) GO. Many of us mistakenly fill in number 4 as STOP, because of the progressive rhymes and the number of spaces provided for an answer. But clearly STOP is not the right answer (you STOP at a RED light, not at a GREEN one). The expectation of rhyme and the immediate assumption that the answer must use four letters lead the viewer astray and ultimately to the wrong answer.

EXERCISE 3 has always been my favorite. I have presented it to hundreds of people individually and in groups and the result is always remarkable. The number of F's in the sentence is ten. I have heard answers ranging from four to eleven, with at least 80% of respondents giving a wrong answer. Some individuals tend to miss the OF's consistently, because of the "V" sound, but this alone does not account for the prevalence of misperception or the wide discrepancy in the number of F's reported. My *ad hoc* research using this exercise has led me to the conclusion that we must bring a healthy dose of humility to our inflated sense of always being right.

Advanced *Homo sapiens*, utilizing their highly evolved perceptual acuity, are unable to count the number of F's in a single sentence.

As a therapist, my starting point is a complete absence of faith in the accuracy of human perception. When clients begin to argue about "what was said three weeks ago" during a heated fight, I urge them to talk in terms of their subjective experience rather than asserting an objective account of what actually took place. I make the assumption that I am dealing with normal human beings who, like myself, aren't even capable of counting F's. If we can accept the dramatic limitations of our perceptions, we can begin to communicate more authentically about our own experiences and make room for the myriad of ways others might experience the same events.

Another key fact about human perception is that the more emotionally charged a situation is, the more our perception tends to be distorted. When the police take an auto accident report and one of the witnesses happens to be the parent of the driver, the parent's account will be more suspect than the observations of an unemotional bystander. When couples get into disputes over emotionally loaded issues (money, sex, in-laws, etc.)—subjects which are charged with intensity—the perceptions of both partners will often be radically skewed. If people cannot even count F's correctly in a totally non-threatening exercise, how can they be trusted to accurately and fully portray the reality of complex, emotionally saturated issues? They can't.

Settling relational problems demands an approach of individual humility as well as mutual respect for perceptual differences.

Awareness and acceptance of our flawed perceptual capacities can lead to a less rigid and authoritative overtone to our verbal assertions. Even small adjustments in our inflection and choice of words can be instrumental in setting the stage for continued communication rather than shutting down discussion with arrogance and accusation. Most partners will be able to respond more openly when we use phrases like:

- *"What I thought I heard you say was . . ."*

- *"The way I see things is . . ."*

- *"It feels to me like . . ."*

- *"I may not be seeing the whole picture, but . . ."*

We can speak as experts of our own viewpoints and subjective experiences without threatening the reality of others. Instead of arguing about what is real, we can share our own unique outlooks and honor the personal perspectives offered by others. Such a shift in attitude is a vital step in developing and sustaining mature respect for our partners.

A pictorial model which emphasizes the limitations of individual perception is offered below.

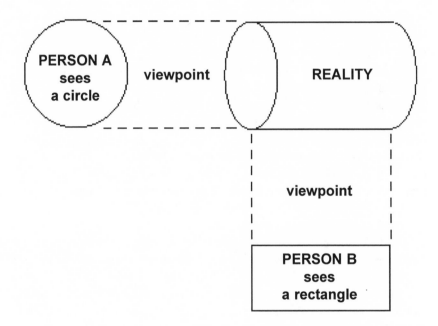

When viewing a three-dimensional cylinder ("REALITY") from varied two-dimensional viewpoints, stunningly different perceptions of reality are possible—all of which are valid. From person A's vantage point, REALITY looks like a circle. Person B, on the other hand, viewing REALITY from a different angle, sees a rectangle. Person A is not visually impaired or insane, nor is Person B hallucinatory or mentally disabled. To each, a particular viewing perspective produces equally valid, though limited conclusions.

The three-dimensional cylinder is, of course, neither a circle nor a rectangle. It is essential for each person to understand that his or her perception is, in fact, an order of magnitude different from the reality of the actual object. If perceptual limitations are granted from the start, each person can share his unique perspective instead of trying to convince the other of who is right and who is wrong. If partners mistakenly judge their personal perception to be ultimate reality, then an argument will likely ensue over whether objective reality is a circle or a rectangle—neither of which is correct. Both partners must realize that the full scope of objective reality is, in truth, never accessible to any human being. The human experience is restricted to "circles" and "rectangles," while the actual "cylinders" that constitute the external world have a breadth and complexity that transcend our meager capacity to comprehend.

The key to finding satisfaction in any relationship is for each person, out of genuine humility, to be willing to step beyond his own perceptual framework to understand the discrepant experience of his partner. Person A needs to accept that Person B sees REALITY as a rectangle, and Person B needs to let go of his viewpoint long enough to acknowledge that Person A sees REALITY as a circle.

Healthy relationships require open-minded understanding of each other's experience and perceptions rather than simply asserting our own singular point of view.

If I can listen to and accept your perceptions as genuine and pertinent, then I create an atmosphere in which you can openly consider *my* way of seeing and understanding. This kind of exchange—steeped in personal respect, patience and a humble recognition of our own limitations—is the essence of relationship. It is the highest expression of intimacy to share ourselves (our thoughts, feelings, perceptions and experiences) with an equal partner who truly values what we share— even if they do not see things the same way or agree with our interpretations. Such loving tolerance is ultimately the key to resolving relational distress and settling emotional debts.

BEING ABSOLUTELY WRONG

Accepting the limitations of our perceptions means that we always need to remain open to the possibility that we can be *wrong*. Being able to *see* when we are wrong and being able to *admit* to ourselves and others that we are wrong is one of the most difficult yet essential elements to a healthy relationship. The tendency is for most of us to make false assumptions or to have distorted perceptions while *believing* and *insisting* that we are absolutely right. It is frightening how rooted in our "rightness" we can be and how tenaciously and dogmatically we can hold on to our viewpoint even in the face of overwhelming evidence against it. Most of us simply do not want to admit that we are wrong no matter what. I can offer a personal example that convinced me years ago of my own propensity for being absolutely wrong at times when I am convinced of being completely right.

About fifteen years ago, I was working under the kitchen sink to repair a broken pipe. Being a fairly incompetent plumber, I had been working for about two hours on what should have been a half-hour job. In that time, I had managed to create more problems than I had fixed. The kitchen had a door that led out to the garage and I had gone back and forth about a half-dozen times to get tools from my workbench. As I was crouched under the sink soaked with garbage disposal water and pipe grease, my wife came home from work. She drove up, parked the car and walked into the kitchen from the garage through the open door.

After saying hello, she delivered the following words, verbatim: "Do you need to leave this door open?" These were her only words.

In my state of frustration and self-condemnation for my plumbing woes, she might as well have hit me in the head with a shovel and said, "You incompetent, insensitive idiot, why don't you get up and close the damned door!"

At an emotional level, that is what I was utterly convinced she had said to me by her words and intonation. I said nothing and she left the room without another word. That was our entire exchange.

About three days later, in the heat of some other argument, I chimed in by saying, "And another thing! It makes me furious when you walk in and deliver those *indirect* messages like you did the other day."

At this point, she looked at me like I was some creature from another world. "What are you talking about?" she asked directly.

I spent the next few minutes describing my experience of her coming home and *telling* me to shut the damned door.

After listening patiently she said, "Listen to me, when I came home the other day, all I did was ask you if you needed to leave the door open. That was it. If you thought that I was either criticizing you or telling you what to do, then you are being paranoid (*note: this was not easy for a psychologist to swallow*). You were reacting to something that simply did not exist. I was only asking because I was going to close the door if you didn't need to keep going out to the garage. Since you said nothing, I just left it open."

I listened to my wife and realized that my options were to trust what she was saying or hold onto my own original belief. To not believe her meant that she was either lying to me, trying to trick me or that she herself was delusional. To accept her account of her own intention and motivation meant accepting that I was wrong in my perception and needed to apologize to *her* for my own false accusation.

I must tell you, a very big, powerful, prideful part of myself resisted believing her. I am a betting man and at the time of the incident, I would have bet everything that I owned that I was absolutely right. The truth was, I was absolutely wrong.

Having grown up in an environment where indirect communication, double-messages and innuendoes were prevalent, it wasn't hard for me or my wife to understand why I heard her words the way that I did. This certainly wasn't the first time that such a distortion in my message reception had occurred—it was more like the ten thousandth. But the degree of my *certainty* in this particular situation ended up scaring me and jarring me into the truth of my own capacity for misinterpreting words, erroneously attributing false motives and digging my heels in about "being right."

Time and again I see this same pattern played out in couples therapy. In order for all of us to get past such distortions and the ensuing relational stalemates, it is essential to be open at all times to the possibility that we might be wrong. When we remain humble and can admit to ourselves and our partners that we might not be right after all, then we create an atmosphere where mutual validation can occur.

MUTUAL DEBT PERCEPTION: THE FIRST STEP TO SETTLEMENT

It is imperative that both partners acknowledge a debt's existence in order for resolution to begin. Partners need not agree about the debt—what constitutes the debt, its origin, its importance, its legitimacy—but both parties must affirm that the debt is indeed real. Remember that our original premise is that a debt is real as soon as one partner perceives that he or she owes something or that something is owed to him or her.

Since a real debt is created when either partner perceives himself or herself as debtor or creditor, the mandatory first step toward resolution requires acknowledging the debt holder's reality. If my partner declares, "I feel like you owe me something for taking care of your mother all these years," I might disagree that the circumstances warrant any claim for repayment. However, my partner's belief that a debt exists, in and of itself, is sufficient to establish the reality of the debt, regardless of my opinion or viewpoint.

Accepting the reality of something does not necessitate granting its validity.

I must be willing to accept my partner's perception that she is a creditor whether or not I feel that her position is justifiable under the circumstances. The key step is for me to affirm my partner's status as creditor and to acknowledge the debt's existence even if I do not agree that the debt is justifiable.

At this point, the only truth that matters is that my partner perceives a debt, therefore a relational debt does indeed exist and needs to be addressed. It is vital that I restrain any impulse to dismiss or disregard my partner's feelings, to argue against the legitimacy of her reality or to try to prove her wrong. I need to put aside seeing reality as only my "circle" and step into my partner's shoes long enough to understand why she sees the same thing as a "rectangle." It is paramount that I listen openly, patiently and in a non-judgmental manner.

Debt acknowledgment can be a monumental challenge, but it is essential to debt resolution.

If I fail to consider your separate point of view, I am ultimately forced into extreme and rash conclusions about you. When I dogmatically adhere to my singular reality, to the utter exclusion of all other perspectives, and you persist in espousing your conflicting point of view, then I can arrive at only one of the following conclusions—you must be:

A) Deluded
B) Lying

C) Crazy

D) All of the above

There are no other choices. So long as I champion my elevated position as sole arbiter of reality, I cannot escape the conclusion that you are seriously defective if you happen to disagree with me. But in making such drastic judgments about you, I poison the interaction with a toxic mixture of distrust, belittlement, condemnation and a sweeping invalidation of the very substance of who you are. Obviously in such an atmosphere there is no potential for any kind of meaningful exchange or resolution.

Therefore, in order to avoid such an emotional stalemate, mutual acknowledgment of diverse realities is imperative. The fact is, what we all need to seek is acknowledgment of our experience by our partners on an equal footing. Going back to our previous example, I must hear and acknowledge that my partner feels a debt is owed to her for taking care of my mother. In the very process of affirming her creditor status, I will have taken a huge step toward resolving the debt. In fact, if an emotional creditor can get his partner to admit the reality of the debt, the creditor will often be satisfied and require no payment at all. In many instances, all the creditor really needs is confirmation that her status as creditor has been recognized. By striving to see and comprehend my partner's viewpoint and internal logic— even if I do not agree with her conclusions—then the primary impediments to resolution are swept away. The type of affirmation I might extend to my partner would be something like:

> *"I can see how you would feel I owe you something for taking care of my mother all of these years. I have always felt it was my duty to have her live with us and so I always saw her presence here as a given. It seemed to me that her financial generosity balanced things out. I never realized that you felt differently. It never occurred to me that I might owe you something in return for your help with her. But if you do feel a debt exists, I'm willing to do what I can to settle things with you. I certainly don't deny that you gave a lot of yourself to help her. What can I do to repay you?"*

Frequently, such an acknowledgment of debt will be met with a response like:

"I guess what I've really wanted all along was for you to realize how much I have done. I've just needed your recognition. It makes me feel better to know that you do understand my position. I guess I don't really want anything more than that."

Genuine understanding and affirmation are the most powerful means for creating deep emotional bonding. All of us want to feel understood and have our thoughts and emotions valued by others, even if they disagree with us. The ability to step outside ourselves and to see, hear and feel the experience of someone else is the touchstone of our humanity.

Relationships are like parking garages; there is usually NO CHARGE with VALIDATION.

TERMS OF SETTLEMENT: SPECIFYING AN AGREEMENT FOR RESOLUTION

Although seeing our partner's point of view is an irreplaceable first step—and sometimes the only necessary step for debt resolution—there are many situations which require a more concrete repayment of the perceived debt. When acknowledgment and validation are not sufficient in and of themselves to discharge a debt, specific terms of settlement must be reached. The terms of settling a debt involve: currencies of payment, the schedule of payment, and consequences for delinquency or default. Clear communication about these issues is essential for establishing a well-defined agreement between both parties. If this phase of negotiation is colored by false assumptions, vague expectations or discrepant interpretations, more problems will be generated than resolved.

Currencies of Payment

Financial debts can be bartered and paid off with a wide spectrum of currencies—anything from dollars to deutsche marks, bushels of wheat to pounds of pork bellies, gold to fertilizer, military equipment to medical aid. Whatever the commodity might be, the key factor for debt liquidation is that it be a form of payment deemed acceptable by the creditor and a commodity within the means of the debtor. It is useless for a creditor to demand cotton from a corn farmer just as it would be futile for a debtor to offer payment in crude oil if gold was the required standard.

Likewise, relational debts can be settled with a wide variety of currencies. The possible tenders are unlimited, but the guiding principle is that the form of payment must be agreed upon by both creditor and debtor. The following list provides some idea of the scope and range of relational currencies.

CURRENCIES FOR SETTLING RELATIONAL DEBTS

TANGIBLE GOODS
Personal Gifts
- Flowers
- Specialty foods and candy
- Special beverages (champagne, wine, coffee)
- Jewelry
- Perfume, cologne
- Apparel and accessories

Personal Tokens
- Notes and cards
- Letter of explanation or apology
- Artistic expressions (photographs, drawings, poems)
- Meaningful books
- Personal tapes, CDs, records

Specified Items
- Money
- Home, apartment
- Furnishings
- Appliances
- Houseware
- Automobile or other vehicles
- Tools and hardware
- Entertainment electronics (TV, VCR, stereo)
- Hobby accouterments (musical instruments, sewing machine)
- Sporting goods

SELECT SERVICES
Personal Intimacies
- Structured time for communication
- Dates and scheduled activities

- Hugs, increased affection
- Massages, back rubs, foot rubs
- Specific sexual favors

Personal Favors

- Errands
- Transportation
- Assumption of responsibility (buying gifts, planning social events)
- Specified tasks (wash partner's car, cook a special dinner)

General Tasks and Responsibilities

- Chores (cleaning, gardening, cooking, shopping)
- Childcare
- Designated projects (paint kitchen, clean out attic, build fence)
- Attend events (business dinner, church, opera)

BEHAVIORAL CHANGES

Cessation of Specified Behaviors

- Stop smoking, stop drinking alcohol
- Give up sweets, fats
- Stop swearing
- Give up specific activity (golf, watching TV, shopping)

Performance of Specified Behaviors

- Lose weight
- Exercise
- Be on time
- Phone calls
- Engage in designated activities (sports, cultural events, hobbies)
- Appearance (get haircut, wear certain clothes, make-up)
- Specified act (go to dentist, start savings account, plan vacation)

SYMBOLIC ACTS OF ATONEMENT

- Relinquish something of value (possession, activity)
- Perform aversive task (wax car, clean gutters, figure taxes)

This listing is far from exhaustive, but it demonstrates the wide variety of potential currencies that can be utilized in dealing with relational debts. As is the case with financial settlements, desirability to the creditor and availability to the debtor are both essential requirements of the tender.

The form of payment must be fully acceptable to the creditor and within the means of the debtor.

Judgments about the nature of payment are irrelevant. Someone might see the requested currency as "bizarre," "silly," "extreme," or "meaningless," but as long as it is sufficient for the creditor and agreeable to the debtor, it is appropriate for debt settlement. Max and Christie provide a good example of how effective debt settlement works.

Although Max and Christie have been married for nineteen years, Max harbored a dark secret. Unknown to his wife, Max had previously been in a marriage which ended in an annulment. He had never told Christie about his past for fear that she would leave him, but recently the truth came out when an unexpected letter from Max's ex-wife arrived at their home. Christie was shocked and devastated. It was a shattering blow to her trust in Max to find out that he had been married before and had never told her.

Through long and painful discussions, Max and Christie both aired their fears, hurts and justifications. Though their marriage was close to tearing apart due to Christie's sense of betrayal, the couple desperately wanted to get beyond this crisis and preserve their commitment to one another.

The first signs of movement occurred when Max articulated his feelings of guilt and his desire to make restitution for his offense. After careful deliberation, Christie came up with three things which she felt would be adequate to resolve her anger and need for restitution. Her requirements for repayment were: 1) that Max give up smoking cigars; 2) that he take over grocery shopping for one year; and 3) that he plant a yellow rose bush in their yard as a symbol of their ever growing love.

Max was baffled by these requests, since they seemed to have no relevance to his act of deceit, but he was more than willing to comply with each. The couple solidified an agreement which specified all the details of payment. As Max followed through with his end of the bargain, Christie's sense of trust was restored and Max was finally liberated from his years of guilt. The debt was settled and the issue put to rest.

Specific forms of payment can be suggested by either the debtor or creditor. The final agreement on the exact currency to be used always must involve both parties—successful liquidation cannot occur with the creditor unilaterally dictating terms or the debtor tendering an unsolicited offer. Both partners must reach a clear agreement on the mode of settlement or the debt will persist.

Often a debtor will attempt to pay off a perceived debt without explicitly announcing to the creditor that repayment is being offered. The risk, of course, is that the payment will go unnoticed and the debtor will be frustrated in his one-sided attempt to escape from debt. The creditor cannot be expected to read the debtor's mind and magically know the intent behind an undeclared offering.

Without an open explanation and agreement, it is likely that the form of currency chosen by the debtor may turn out to be unacceptable to the creditor and thus ineffectual at resolving the debt. Such futile gestures can be so disheartening to the well-intentioned debtor that any future effort to repay will evaporate into a sense of defeat, hopelessness and ultimately resentment. Lawrence and Victoria aptly illustrate just such a situation.

When Lawrence asked Victoria to marry him, he knew full well that he would have to give up his prized Yorkshire Terrier show dog. Victoria's severe allergy to all dogs precluded any possibility of her living in a house which included a canine. Even though Lawrence had raised his beloved Yorkie from a pup, Lawrence had maturely evaluated the situation and clearly chose his marriage to Victoria as the most important thing to him.

Just prior to their wedding, Lawrence gave his dog to a respected breeder. The separation was emotional and difficult, but he felt resolved to the necessary decision.

Victoria, however, clung onto a nagging guilt over depriving Lawrence of his long-term companion as well as his passionate hobby for showing dogs. She knew in her rational mind that she was not to blame for her uncontrollable allergies, but she still felt in debt for Lawrence's sacrifice.

In her first attempt to repay her perceived debt, Victoria began setting up their home together by taking special care to prominently display the ribbons and trophies which Lawrence's dog had won. Lawrence was actually pained by these constant reminders of his pet, but he never expressed his feelings to Victoria.

His failure to acknowledge her gesture drove Victoria to proffer further payment. On his birthday, she proudly presented him with an oil painting of his prized Yorkshire. After silently staring at the portrait for several long moments, Lawrence broke down into uncontrollable tears.

"I know you mean well," he said to her as he cried, "but you have to stop tormenting me with memories of Angus. I was willing to give him up and I just want to be done with it."

Victoria was truly shocked by her husband's reaction and responded, "I'm sorry, Lawrence. I have felt so guilty for taking him away from you. I feel like I have to do something."

"Look, Victoria," Lawrence responded, "I don't expect anything from you. I made my choice and I have never regretted it. You don't owe me a thing. I wish you would just let it go."

By insisting on tendering repayment in an unacceptable form, Victoria not only failed to extinguish her own guilt but actually made the situation worse. If she had openly disclosed her ongoing guilt and had explored agreeable options for repayment with Lawrence first, her futile efforts and Lawrence's anguish would have been avoided.

The form of currency must be mutually agreeable to the creditor and the debtor for it to be effective tender.

Specificity is essential in determining the proper currency. It is not enough to say, "I want you to repay me with a new car." The year, make, model, color, and options all need to be defined if they are important to the creditor. Similarly, if behavioral change is the requested currency, it needs to be set forth in terms that are crystal clear to both parties. Vague demands such as those which follow will serve only to create confusion:

- *"I want you to try to be more understanding."*

- *"I want you to be more affectionate."*

- *"I want you to show me that you love me."*

- *"I need you to be more sensitive to my needs."*

Imprecise desires need to be translated into specific language, such as:

- *"When I tell you something, I want you to give me your full attention and reflect back to me what you hear me saying."*

- *"I want you to hug and kiss me hello and good-bye each day and hold me and stroke my hair each night before we go to sleep."*

- *"I want you to leave me handwritten notes that express your love for me."*

- *"I want you to ask me each day how I am feeling and to leave the television off while we have dinner together."*

Such specificity usually evokes our old nemesis of wanting our partners to be clairvoyant and magically know exactly what we want without any need for a clear expression of our desire. The idea of explicitly voicing relational needs or wants is often shunned because it seems so structured and stilted. The common rebuttals are:

- *"If I have to tell her what I want, it isn't the same."*

- *"I want him to want to do it, not just do it because I asked."*

- *"It has to be spontaneous—asking takes away all the magic."*

Unfortunately, it is an inescapable fact of life that our partners cannot read our minds or mystically intuit our needs on any consistent basis. Even if they "get it right" nine times out of ten, it is the tenth one that always lodges in our psyche and tears at our gut. It may not fuel our romantic fantasies to verbalize our expectations clearly, but explicit communication is ultimately the only pathway to a deep mutual understanding and ongoing intimate connection. True satisfaction can only arise from the passionate bonds that develop between partners who take the risk of fully revealing their hearts in the presence of someone they trust.

Schedule of Payment

Once the form of currency has been established for a debt settlement, a time frame for payment must be negotiated. Relational debts can be paid off in one lump sum or over time with a designated schedule of payments. Often the type of currency will dictate the reimbursement schedule. If, for instance, a creditor and debtor agree to "one year of mowing the lawn" as the currency of repayment, then each week of lawn mowing will constitute one of fifty-two payment installments. If the terms of repayment call for the purchase of a new fishing rod, then the debt will be settled upon purchase and delivery of the single item. The appropriate schedule of payment is purely a function of what the creditor and debtor agree to. The *schedule* of payment, like the *form* of payment, must be set forth clearly and definitively.

Penalties for Delinquency or Default

The final provision of an agreement for debt repayment involves specified consequences in the event that the debtor is delinquent with payment or defaults entirely. It solidifies the agreement to predetermine the penalties assessed for delinquency or default so that the settlement maintains a sense of fairness and integrity. For instance, a debt settlement between Allen and Becky incorporated the following key penalty clause:

> Allen *(debtor)* agrees to be home from work no later than 6:30 P.M. each work night for the next six months. Failure to be home on time, within a five-minute grace period as measured by the kitchen clock, will result in Allen owing Becky a back rub for the same number of minutes he is late. Becky may accumulate minutes and request a back-rub at her discretion.

The back-rub contingency promotes a sense of fairness and security in the couple's debt settlement. Becky has more faith in the agreement knowing the consequence if Allen does not follow through with his commitment to come home on time. Allen is willing to go along with what he perceives to be a reasonable penalty should he fail to keep up his end of the bargain.

While the possibility of delinquency can be anticipated and appropriately penalized, total default requires a complete reworking of the debt settlement agreement. Default is always an indicator that the original agreement was fatally flawed in some way. Abject failure to fulfill the requirements of settlement might be a function of:

- The debtor lying about his commitment to the agreement.

- The debtor failing to assess the cost of compliance.

- The form of currency turning out to be beyond the debtor's means.

- The schedule of payment proving unworkable.

- The debtor simply changing his mind midstream.

Regardless of the reason behind the breach, a defaulted agreement inevitably means going back to square one—redefining the debt, reviewing the appropriateness and acceptability of the currency, mapping out a settlement agreement, and insuring that the debtor has sufficiently committed himself to the designated path of resolution. Agreements which are truly acceptable and genuinely embraced by both parties will always be fulfilled. A broken agreement should be viewed as an indication that the agreement itself was flawed, and should not be used as a weapon or indictment by one party against the other. The spotlight of failure needs to be shined on the agreement, not the participants.

The Value of a Written Agreement
To assure mutual understanding, to remove any ambiguity about the important details and to create an indisputable record of the final terms of settlement, debt resolution agreements should always be put

in writing. Let's not forget, many emotional debts arise initially because of false assumptions, misperceptions and discrepant interpretations of the same circumstances. At the moment of debt settlement, it is foolhardy to rely on the same limited powers of perception, imprecise communication and distorted memory which were responsible for creating the problems in the first place.

**It makes no sense to try smoothing out
a piece of wood with the same sander
that marred the surface in the first place.**

Writing out a settlement agreement is a simple process which can avoid complicated and heated disputes that start with plaintive cries such as:

- *"That's not what I agreed to."*

- *"I don't remember it that way."*

- *"There you go twisting the facts again."*

- *"I thought we already agreed—why do you keep trying to renegotiate?"*

With a written agreement, a tangible record exists to ward off potential misunderstandings. Also, an additional benefit to writing out an agreement is that the process forces both parties to be clear, concise and complete. Committing words to paper is an entirely different experience than verbally discussing an issue. The crucial role and value of written contracts are indisputable in all business transactions, and intimate relationships have no less a need for an objective record of promises, expectations and agreements. Couples who are willing to complete the communication process by committing themselves in writing will achieve a far higher level of certainty that their agreements properly express their own fully explored individual needs as well as their shared goals together.

To be effective, a written relational debt settlement agreement can be surprisingly short and simple. Its elegance lies not in complex or verbose phraseology, but in concise structure and plain language. The following sample format incorporates all the elements of an effective agreement.

DEBT SETTLEMENT AGREEMENT

This debt settlement agreement is hereby made between:

_____ *(Debtor)* and _____ *(Creditor)*

The purpose of the agreement is to fully resolve the debt between the parties which arose over the issue of: _____

_____

As full and final compensation, Debtor agrees to pay and Creditor agrees to accept payment in the form of (specify currency): _____

_____

Debtor and Creditor further agree to the following schedule of payment: _____

_____

_____

_____

Furthermore, in the event of delinquency, Debtor agrees to the following consequences: _____

_____

_____

_____	_____
Debtor's Signature	Date
_____	_____
Creditor's Signature	Date

**If an agreement is worth making,
it is worth committing to writing—
never let superficial romantic notions
cloud the issue of clarity.**

Many couples initially balk at the idea of putting their agreements in writing, but I have never seen partners who regretted either going through the process or having the security of an objective record. Having taken the time and energy required to commit their agreements to writing, even reticent individuals become utterly convinced of the value of the experience and the solidity of the end product. Agreements between partners end up being true reflections of their intentions. Among the frequent comments I have heard are:

- *"It forced us to be direct about what we wanted."*

- *"By writing things down we became aware for the first time of what our conflicts really were."*

- *"We both felt more secure when we put it down in black and white."*

- *"It's nice to know what the rules are."*

Committing our innermost hopes and needs to paper might offend our sense of ethereal love. However, there is nothing romantic about the bickering, accusations and hurt feelings which result from a lack of clarity. A reliance on mind reading to conjure up magical romance is destined to lead to disappointment and heartbreak. Romantic illusion will ultimately crash rudely into the finite limits of our human nature—we are not magicians or telepathic white knights capable of riding in on a gleaming charger to nobly satisfy our partner's every desire at each critical moment. Magic is an enchanting notion, but it can never sustain a flesh-and-blood relationship.

The direct expression of our human needs and desires is the real path to true romance.

---

* A SPECIAL MESSAGE TO THE HOPELESS ROMANTIC *

If you are enamored with the idealistic notion of perfect love, you may be utterly convinced that the coldness of straightforward requests or the austerity of written agreements to settle disputes will always spoil the freshness and magic of glowing romance. But clarity and specificity are in no way antithetical to warmth and passion in an authentic expression of love.

Your mental picture of clear communication probably suggests some kind of abrupt, sterile demand followed immediately by an obligatory, robotic response from the dutiful partner. Rest assured, the real experience of expressing needs is vastly different than what your fears portray.

Indeed, there may be initial discomfort for both partners when desires are first voiced. But the awkwardness soon dissipates as the process of verbalizing our needs is gradually integrated into the daily fabric of our relationship and becomes second nature. This integration evolves in two key ways.

First, the art of requesting grows to be more natural and fluid with practice. As we get what we want more consistently, the effectiveness of asking begins to reinforce itself. Furthermore, we also come to experience the affirming and connective quality that accompanies honest self-expression.

Secondly, by having the chance to see our partner's specific requests, we are able to enter into a deeper understanding of the rhythms and nature of our partner's true desires and needs. As time passes, our developing intimate knowledge of our partner's inner life allows for the possibility of the very sensitivity and spontaneity which the ideal of romantic love promised in the first place. The amazing paradox is that the more we learn to ask, the less we *have* to ask. As we reveal ourselves to one another, our accumulated knowledge forms a base for free-flowing, intuitive giving—but our intuitions are now rooted in fact and experience instead of blind guesswork or magic.

The following vignette demonstrates the kind of enriched romance that can spring from clear communication between partners.

Jillian brought her husband Scott to therapy after a year of marital frustration. To Jillian, Scott seemed to be quietly disgruntled and punctuated his pouting with sporadic outbursts of biting sarcasm. Try as she might, she had been unsuccessful at prying out the reasons for his cold withdrawal.

Jillian described her experience of daily life with Scott. "He used to be so attentive and caring. I don't understand what's happened. I married him because of his warmth and passion, but now everything feels frozen. He almost seems to disdain me and I don't know why. Scott, why can't you just tell me why you're treating me this way?"

Scott brooded in silence for several long moments and then blurted out his frustration. "Damn it, that's exactly the problem! Why do I always have to spell everything out for you? I can't believe how blind you are. Why it is that I have to initiate everything in this relationship?"

At this point, it was important to direct Scott's outburst toward the heart of his frustration. Scott talked around several complaints before he arrived at his central issue—their sexual relationship.

"Every time we have sex," he stated, "it's only because I'm the one who makes it happen. Jillian never once has shown any interest in getting things started. If it weren't for me pushing the issue, we'd never have sex. How am I supposed to feel, living with someone who obviously has no interest in me?" Scott's disclosure opened up a dialogue.

"How can you say that, Scott? I love making love with you." Jillian's voice was anguished.

Scott's eyebrows went up. "Well, that's news to me. If you like it so much, then why don't you ever approach me first? Why does it always feel like I'm twisting your arm?"

"I had no idea you expected me to ever initiate sex with you," Jillian said.

"That's just it, I don't *expect* you to. I want you to," Scott replied.

Jillian interjected, "Well, why haven't you told me? I don't think I would have any problem initiating, but frankly, it never occurred to me."

"Don't you understand, Jillian," Scott kept his eyes riveted on a spot on the wall. "If I have to ask you to initiate, that just wrecks the whole thing. I can't think of anything less romantic than instructing you to ask me for sex."

"Well, how am I supposed to know what you want from me if you don't tell me? This is the first time you've ever said anything about this."

It was time for me to step in. "So, Jillian, it sounds like you would be willing to initiate sex with Scott?"

"Of course I would. I really don't have any problem with that."

Scott bit his lip pensively. "Well, it's too late now," he announced, "If you approached me now it would only be because I broke down and asked—it would feel so artificial and contrived."

I wanted both of them to give their relationship a chance to flourish with new rules. "Scott," I began, "you need to understand that Jillian is willing to initiate sex because she really does care about you. You can't dismiss her willingness and love on the basis of her inability to read your mind. Now that she knows what you want, why not let her initiate in her own time and way, and accept it as a genuine gesture of caring for you."

Jillian looked at her partner affectionately, "I wouldn't do this unless I really wanted to. I love you Scott and I want you to know it."

Scott's inflated romantic notions precluded him from giving clear voice to his desire for sexual assertiveness from of his spouse. His self-defeating refusal to ask directly for what he wanted led to a no-win situation that left the couple frustrated and disconnected. The self-fulfilling irony is that Jillian shows genuine interest in being the initiator, but Scott undercuts her enthusiasm with his belief that asking somehow taints her expression of care. Scott's starry-eyed vision of romance ends up delivering the most unromantic consequences of all—unmet needs, unfulfilled desires, mutual frustration and months of bitter alienation.

Fortunately, Scott did make an effort to let Jillian demonstrate her affection toward him. Several weeks after their emotional session, the couple returned to report a dramatic turnaround. Jillian had indeed chosen an appropriate time to instigate a sexual encounter with Scott. Though Scott found it awkward at first to accept her advance, he soon was swept up in the experience and his impulse to dismiss her willingness was quickly forgotten. As time went by, Scott no longer questioned Jillian's initiatives and was able to accept them as spontaneous expressions of her desire and care. In the end, both partners reported an exciting increase in their romantic feelings for one another.

Even Hopeless Romantics can find true romance—but only when they are willing to ask.

CONCLUSION

Emotional debt resolution must always begin by an acknowledgment of the debt by both parties. Even if one person finds the debt ridiculous or unjustifiable, he must be willing to acknowledge that it exists for his partner. Because of the distortions inherent in human perception, partners must communicate clearly and specifically to insure a "mutual debt perception"—the first step in any debt settlement. Once the debt is mutually understood and acknowledged, the terms of settlement can be negotiated in a "currency" which is both available to the emotional debtor and acceptable to the emotional creditor. Along with the form of currency, a "schedule of payment" and the specific consequences or "penalties for default" should be agreed upon.

The value of committing the entire "debt settlement" to writing cannot be stressed enough. The clarity and endurance of a written agreement allows future misunderstandings to be examined in the light of an established record. The *process* of working out a written agreement together virtually always results in not only clarity but also a positive sense of teamwork. Even though some "romantics" may find the idea of a written agreement a bit stringent, it has been my experience with many couples that the actual process and result will fuel greater intimacy and love.

Chapter 7

ᴨᴇGOᴛᴛᴀᴛᴛᴨG DᴇBᴛ SᴇᴛᴛᴸᴇᴍᴇᴨᴛS
The Art of Open Exchange

*How absolute the Knave is! we must speak by the
card or equivocation will undo us.*

- Shakespeare

One frequent situation I am presented with as a couples therapist
occurs when partners come to the first appointment looking sheepish
and introduce their purpose in the following way.

> "I'm sure you see some pretty horrible marriage situ-
> ations," Cheryl begins, "but we're not like that at all."
>
> "That's right, Doctor, neither of us are alcoholics or
> child abusers," adds George with a nervous smile. "Nothing
> serious like that."
>
> "We've been together for eleven years now and basi-
> cally have a really good marriage and love each other a
> lot," Cheryl continues. "Our problem is that we just don't
> communicate."

It is astounding how often the phrase, *"we just don't communicate,"* is offered by partners as a description of their relationship's
central problem. In the early years of my practice, I would adopt the
couple's mind-set and rush to problem-solve the communication defi-
ciencies with an arsenal of interventions ranging from active listening

exercises to intensive explorations into the anxieties blocking the spontaneous expression of ideas, feelings, needs and desires.

After counseling hundreds of couples, however, I have come to realize that non-communication should not be viewed as a problem crying out for immediate resolution. In fact, the failure to openly communicate usually serves a very important role in the relationship—non-communication actually protects, insulates and preserves the fragile balance of the relationship.

I am now less willing to promote or force change until the risks of improving communication are understood and accepted. Just as individuals have psychological defense mechanisms (e.g. denial, rationalization, projection, sublimation) that serve to protect them from perceived or unconscious threats, relationships also develop modes of defense. I am convinced that non-communication (and all of its variations) is the most prevalent of all relational defense mechanisms. A lack of communication is almost always the result of partners colluding, consciously or unconsciously, in an effort to protect the relationship from potential harm or even permanent destruction.

Non-communication is a relational
defense mechanism that can safeguard
a relationship against probable friction
and potential devastation.

Once non-communication is viewed as a defense mechanism, then as a therapist, I must be very careful and respectful of the purpose it is serving. In the same way that a competent therapist will not rush in and tear away the defensive structure that serves to protect an individual client, the process of confronting the defense mechanism of a couple should be approached delicately. The goal cannot simply be to rush the two people toward effective communication. The process of confrontation and change requires trust, motivation, clarity and an awareness of the potential benefits and risks inherent in the process of change. These days, when couples come to me presenting non-communication as their central problem, I usually respond by saying something along the following lines.

"I'm certainly willing to help you improve the communication in your relationship, but let's be clear about what we mean by good communication and what the potential risks are of implementing it. My picture of good communication involves two people who are connected to their own individual thoughts and feelings and who are able and willing to express these to one another openly, clearly and in a way that is congruent with how they actually think and feel.

My experience is that partners often don't communicate in this manner because either one or both partners are detached from their own emotions and desires or, more commonly, they do not feel it is safe to openly express themselves in the arena of their relationship. Just imagine for a moment what things would be like if both of you woke up tomorrow and suddenly started to communicate in the manner which I am describing. Each of you would have clarity about what you truly think and feel and you would begin to express your ideas, opinions, desires and emotions directly and openly to one another. What do you think the risks might be to both you and the relationship if this were to happen?

Couples are usually thrown off balance by approaching the idea of open communication in terms of "risks." They have already assumed that open communication can only mean something constructive, something positive. Their idealized premise is that good communication always brings closeness, joy, understanding and intimacy. However, let's go back to the definition of good communication that I am proposing:

> Good communication consists of people being aware of their thoughts and feelings, and being willing to express these in an open, direct and congruent way.

While couples may anticipate growth and bonding, the actual experience of self-revelation is more apt to produce turmoil. My experience, unlike the presupposition of many couples, is that honest and direct communication can result in all hell breaking loose. We must be cognizant that there are numerous risks associated with revealing our true selves. When we contemplate aloud and expose our unmitigated desires to our partners, many fears may flood our minds such as:

- She'll think I'm perverted.

- I know he'll be mad if I tell him.

- What if she laughs at me?

- I don't think he'll really take me seriously.

- I'll be so embarrassed or humiliated.

- She'll get upset and it could lead to a major blow-up.

- He'll use what I tell him against me and try to leverage his position.

In fact, when partners begin to fully express their authentic thoughts and feelings the result is almost always some degree of conflict. The conflict may be big or small, old or new, trivial or intense, conscious or unconscious—but the result of good communication is ultimately going to expose differences between partners.

Each individual in a relationship is a distinct, separate person with his and her own unique set of ideas, values and emotions that mean differences between partners. This is a given. The existence of differences mandates some degree of disparity, disagreement, and opposition. On this level, I am defining conflict as *divergence* rather than *hostility*. Within this meaning, conflict thus describes a *difference* of opinions, *contrary* desires, a *diversity* of perspectives, a *disparity* of needs—not antagonism, assault and warfare. Individuality means differences, and a relationship between emotionally strong, differentiated individuals is always colored by some incompatible ideas and needs.

When partners begin to voice their genuine feelings, surprises of all magnitudes can abound.

- "I have always hated the flannel pajamas she wears to bed."

- "I know he thinks I love his famous pot roast, but each time I have to eat it I nearly gag."

- "I've put up with his mother for all this time just to make him happy."

- "If he really wants to know how I felt about the anniversary present he gave me, the truth is I couldn't have been more disappointed"

- "To be honest, I'm not sure that I really do love her any more."

Much of our communication is filtered or suppressed, because we can already anticipate the negative reactions that will ensue if we open our mouths and dare to utter our authentic feelings. Expressions such as the ones given above are not likely to bring about joy, closeness and intimacy. Such utterances are far more liable to result in hurt, disappointment, astonishment and anger. Partners on the receiving end usually respond with a sense of indignation and betrayal.

- "I can't believe what I'm hearing."

- "How can you feel that way?"

- "I always thought that you liked the way I . . ."

- "I'm totally crushed."

- "Well it's about time you fessed up to the truth."

- "Why haven't you ever said anything before?"

In the film, *A Few Good Men*, Jack Nicholson delivers one of his memorable lines to Tom Cruise during a stirring courtroom scene. At one dramatic point Tom Cruise screams at Nicholson, "I want the TRUTH!" and Nicholson shoots back, **"You can't handle the truth!"** This is the operative attitude many partners adopt—we don't think our spouses can accept the truth and we aren't confident that our relationships can withstand the harsh realities that the truth may reveal. Therefore, what is real and genuine often gets buried or radically filtered as a means of protecting us, our partners and our relationships from the potential ravages of conflict.

We are not confident that our partners or our relationships can tolerate the TRUTH.

In order for the truth to emerge, for open communication to be risked, a relationship must have a basis of trust, commitment, mutual respect and love. Beyond these basic qualities of a relationship, three additional factors are necessary to successfully address conflict: 1) couples must have an appreciation for and an acceptance of their differences; 2) they must recognize the inevitability of some conflict in their relationship; and, 3) they must have confidence in their abilities to effectively deal with conflict in a productive and mutually satisfying way. All too often, conflict is feared, detested and thus avoided at all costs. It is viewed like a life-threatening disease and couples go to great lengths to prevent its outbreak. Yet conflict is not only unavoidable in healthy relationships, it is **essential** to them.

Healthy communication identifies and spotlights conflict as we have defined it. Therefore, a prerequisite of good communication is for couples to have the capacity, motivation, and tenacity to embrace and work through their differences as their unique personalities emerge in their relationships.

When partners feel confident in their abilities to face and productively contend with disparities and disagreements, they have far less need to either fear or avoid conflict. Instead, they can accept conflict as a natural, normal part of their relationships and function together in ways that promote win-win resolutions.

Differences between individuals are inevitable in any relationship, and healthy communication serves to illuminate rather than cover up such conflict.

PARTNERS VERSUS OPPONENTS

Individuals in a relationship, at any given point in time, function in one of two ways. Either they work together as collaborative **partners** or they battle each other as **opponents**. *Partners* have a sense of being teammates—united on the same side, working towards common goals and supporting one another through shared adversities. Partners feel connected, accepted, supported and secure.

Opponents, on the other hand, feel they are on opposite sides trying to overcome one another in an effort to succeed in their own purposes. Opponents feel alone, competitive, suspicious and distrustful of one another.

I often stop couples during a session and ask each of them to assess which mode they feel they are operating in. There never seems to be any hesitation in the answers they give. Each of us knows immediately and instinctively whether we are relating as partners or opponents.

The distinguishing indicators of two opponents fighting one another to get his or her own way are illustrated in the following situation.

Trudy turned to Don while eating dinner and said, "I called up the landscape company today and asked them to come out and lay the sod in our front yard. They'll be here on Wednesday."

Don looked up in disbelief, "You did what?"

"You heard me," said Trudy looking down at her plate as she continued eating.

"We already talked about this," said Don. "We decided that I would handle putting in the new lawn."

Trudy was unfazed. "*You* decided that *you* would put in the lawn. Besides, that was three weeks ago, and the last time I looked out front, the only things sprouting were dandelions. I told you that I needed that grass in before the rains start. The kids will be tracking in mud every day if the front yard stays the way it is."

Don rolled his eyes and replied adamantly, "I told you I would get to it. I'm still trying to re-paint the family room like you wanted me to. My God, I only have so much time to get everything done around here."

"Exactly," said Trudy calmly, "that's why I am going to hire some help for a change."

"We don't have the money to be overpaying strangers to come out here and wreck our property. If I do the job, at least it will be done right."

"We don't have the money to be cleaning carpets every week either," replied Trudy. "This is a competent landscape company. They can do a perfectly fine job."

Don was getting exasperated. "They'll screw it up, Trudy, believe me. You can't just 'lay down sod.' That soil has to be roto-tilled and enriched, all of the old weeds have to be eliminated, the sprinkler system has to be designed and put in, the edge stones need to be set...It's not as easy as you think."

"Well, Mister Expert, I'm not going to wait around any longer," Trudy said firmly. "I've already called the landscape company and the lawn *will* go in on Wednesday!"

Don went into a rage, "Well, you sure as hell better figure out a way to pay for it then, Trudy, because I'm not writing out any damned checks!" Don left the room and slammed the door behind him.

The argument between Don and Trudy could be the script of a boxing bout. The two opponents enter the ring, the bell sounds and the fight is on. Trudy jabs— **"I called the landscape company."** Don counters and throws a right hook— **"*I'm* putting in the lawn!"** Trudy comes back with a combination— **"I don't see any lawn out there and I'm not going to have the kids tracking in mud all winter."** Don staggers but comes back with a vicious left to the body followed by an uppercut to the head— **"You can't trust the landscape people and the job involves much more than you think."** Trudy delivers a low blow— **"Mister Expert"** and then forces her opponent into the corner— **"the lawn *will* be put in on Wednesday."** Don lashes back with a brutal left— **"I'm not paying for it!"** The bell sounds, the first round is over, and both bloodied fighters return to their corners.

Neither Don nor Trudy emerged victorious—neither got what he or she wanted and both are emotionally battered in the exchange. As opponents, they have no need to show any compassion or understanding of one another. There is no concern for the validity of the opponent's desires or needs. All that is important is winning.

When *partners* approach conflicts in their relationship, they do so with an attitude of working together for the common good. They view the task of conflict resolution as their challenge, rather than seeing one another as the enemy. *Partners* accept conflict as a natural outgrowth of their differences and work as a team to find creative solutions to preserve and improve the quality of the relationship. Partners understand that conflict resolution takes time, energy, compassion, respect, patience, and perseverance. They are willing to tolerate the discomfort and pain that so often accompany discrepancies, because they truly care about how one another thinks and feels. They are committed to a path of genuine understanding and mutual accommodation.

As a contrast, let's consider how Don and Trudy might address the same issue of putting in a lawn from the perspective of partners instead of opponents.

Trudy turned to Don while eating dinner and said, "Don, it's been three weeks since we talked about putting in the front lawn. I need to have it done soon before the rains start."

"Look, Trudy," Don replied, "I haven't finished painting the family room. I know you're anxious to get the lawn in, but there's only so much I can do at once. Can't you just live with the front yard as it is for a little while longer?"

"I'm not sure I can. Once the rain starts, the kids will be tracking in mud and that will drive me crazy. Why can't we hire out the work to a landscape company and just get it over with?"

Don felt himself tense up as he responded, "Well, paying money we don't have for a job that I can do will drive me crazy. Besides, Trudy, I don't think you realize what we're talking about here—you can't just lay down sod. There's the roto-tilling and weeding, ground preparation, sprinkler system and stone work. You know me, I don't trust anybody to do the work the way I know it needs to be done."

"Well, can't we figure out some way to make it happen sooner?" pleaded Trudy. "I'm willing to try to be patient, but not through the entire winter. What if we hired out some of the heavy preparation work and then you could do the other parts the way you want."

"I'd be willing to pay up to a maximum of three hundred dollars if you find somebody to roto-till and deliver new top soil," said Don.

Trudy thought a moment and asked, "If I get that done this week, would you be willing to put the rest of the painting on hold and work on the front yard this weekend?"

"I could do that, Trudy," replied Don, "but, the whole project will take at least two full weekends, maybe even longer."

"Look, I'd be elated if we have it all finished in the next four weeks," Trudy said. "I'm not trying to be a nag, it's just important to me to get the lawn in before our house becomes a muddy mess."

"I'm happy to postpone the painting and concentrate on the yard, Trudy. I just don't want to spend money foolishly or have the project screwed up when I know how it should be done. You line up the preparation work and I promise you'll have a beautiful lawn by Thanksgiving."

This time, Trudy and Don still have a conflict of opinions, but they approach one another as partners and work together toward a mutually agreeable plan of action. Each person is willing to listen and show respect for the needs of the other. In such a case, there is a spirit of mutual consideration and collaboration which guides the discussion toward a "win-win" resolution. Instead of fighting each other as opponents, Don and Trudy are united as partners in the pursuit of a solution that takes into account both of their needs.

An essential prerequisite of working together as teammates is a spirit of flexibility. Each partner must be willing to consider a number of alternatives if the process of creating a win-win solution is to get off the ground. It is human nature to want to have our own point of view prevail, but being right is often antithetical to getting the very thing we want. If both partners place the highest premium on working together to achieve a mutually satisfying outcome, then their new attitudes can move them towards their desired goal. For instance, if my desired outcome is to have my partner help me prepare dinner, I may thwart receiving the very help I want by insisting that the soup be seasoned the "right way"—meaning my way. Even if the experts support my position on the correct use of seasonings, my need to be right will most likely interfere with getting the help I want. I need to make the choice: is it more important for me to be right or to have my mate help out? In a loving relationship, it is usually more constructive to consciously ratchet down the intensity of needing to be right or to simply prove my point. Instead, the perspective of working together to achieve mutual goals is ultimately the end both partners should unite to gain.

**Partners should put their energies
toward achieving a desired outcome.**

For people to effectively handle conflict as *partners*, there must be a foundation of trust in the relationship. Not only must each partner trust the other to be honest and open, but they also must believe that each of their interests and well-being will be considered and honored by the other. I must have a sense that my partner ultimately cares about my opinions, attitudes and aspirations even in the face of the fact that she may disagree and desire to do things differently. I need to feel that my partner's commitment to me is greater than her commitment to simply getting her own way. We each must feel that the *relationship* takes precedence over our *individual* need for control, power and victory.

Being a partner, however, doesn't mean committing *identity suicide*. The goal is not to sacrifice my wants and needs at every turn as a means of conflict resolution. Instead, being a partner means embracing my needs as well as embracing those of my significant other. It means facing the realities of conflict and pushing ahead together to find ways that account for each of our needs. Being a partner requires an overall attitude and commitment to creating a relationship that has room for both participants to fulfill their individual personhood to the highest level possible. It is a commitment to me being me, you being you and we being the best we can possibly be.

**In the context of commitment and safety,
partners create a relationship with room
for each person to truly be himself or herself.**

MODES OF NEGOTIATING

There are two basic ways that people can negotiate. The first is what I refer to as *"playing poker."* In a "poker game," friendly or not, opponents come to the table with all of their skills and experience directed to strategically defeating one another. Players carefully observe the tactics of the opposition and try to anticipate the overall strategy of each rival. As a poker player, my methods are to bet, raise and bluff, all as a means of achieving my ultimate goal of victory. I can play with various degrees of finesse, deception or ruthlessness, but the game always has one overriding goal—I win and you lose.

There are many negotiations in life that play out like a poker game: the purchase of a home, the buy-out of a company, the trade of a professional baseball player, the haggling at a flea market. Such situations almost always unfold as a strategic match between bargaining opponents, each trying to cut the most advantageous deal for himself. Negotiating can become a very competitive, cut-throat experience, since the ground rules are rooted in self-interest and the ultimate goal is winning: getting exactly what you want by defeating your opposition in any way possible within the sanctioned rules of the game.

There is not anything inherently wrong or evil about the "poker playing" method of negotiating. As long as both parties are willing to accept a strategic approach to the bargaining, then manipulation, slick maneuvering and deception are all accepted and expected. If I go to an automobile dealership to purchase a new car, I walk in expecting a situation where "playing poker" is the established method of negotiating. I know that the salesperson I deal with has some latitude concerning the car price, options, accessories, terms of financing, and potential trade-in value of my current vehicle. I fully expect him to quote me a high price and then to bargain down in a way that he thinks will make me feel I am getting a great deal. I know that he is no fool and that he makes a living driving the hardest bargains he possibly can (in his favor, of course), because ultimately his commission will be based on his ability to woo me into a high price with as many extras and warranty add-ons as he can sell. The salesperson may initially try to convince me of his honesty, trust-worthiness and good intentions to protect *my* interests, but I need to take his words with many grains of salt. I can hear him approaching now:

> "Hello, my friend, and you are my friend. I see you are looking at the new Mustang. A fine, fine choice if I may say so. I can tell right off that you are a man who really knows his cars.
>
> "Well, I'm not supposed to let customers know this . . . so this is just between you and me . . . but since you look like a person I can trust, here's the gospel truth. Since it is the second Tuesday before the end of our third quarter inventory close-out, I can give you this precision automobile for an additional fifteen percent off. All you have to do is purchase the seven year extended warranty and finance through our special home office terms. Please don't let my manager know I let you in on this, but I really want to help you drive away in this automobile today. I want to make your dream come true."

From the start I know I am in a "poker game"; so I am neither gullible to nor offended by the load of horse manure that has so altru-istically been shoveled in my direction. Instead I size up the situation as best I can and counter with my own betting tactics:

"Well, I must admit, it certainly is a gorgeous car . . . but I'm quite sure it's well beyond my price range. I'm wondering, though, if I were to skip financing and write out a check today, would you be able to still give me that fifteen percent off, but on the other special limited edition model, and throw in leather, a sound system upgrade, as well as a three thousand dollar trade-in on my eighty-three Honda like the dealer in Milbrae offered?"

"I'll see your ten dollars and raise you twenty." I have made my opening bet and the "poker game" is on. Perhaps two hours later, after we have haggled over price, options and terms; after he has taken three offers into his manager's office and returned with a counter that each time he assures me is "the absolute lowest he can go;" after I have been saturated with coffee and doughnuts; after I have told him for the fifth time about the two kids I have to put through college; and after just one more test drive—after all that, we may finally settle the deal. The salesperson and I will have played every card we could and each of us will settle only when there is a sense that we have negotiated a deal with which each of us can live. If we can strike an agreement, then I will drive away with my brand new car and he will walk away with his well earned commission.

If, however, our positions are too far apart to arrive at an agreement and either of us reaches a threshold where we are not willing to budge any further, then a stalemate will ensue and the process of negotiation will break down and come to an end. I will trudge off to the next dealership looking for a better deal and the salesperson will regroup for his assault on the next prospective customer who comes through the door.

When it comes to the "poker game" style of negotiating, certain people love it and thrive on it while others detest it entirely. Some people, such as agents, attorneys and sales representatives, make their living "playing poker," but other people either hate the game or feel that they are not very competent at it. These poker disdainers simply refuse to ever go to a garage sale, or street market or even a car dealership. They will often say things like:

- *"I can't stand the thought of haggling."*

- *"The whole sales business is such a game, and I'm not interested in wasting my time playing it."*

- *"Just tell me a fair price and I'll pay it."*

- *"Why should I buy something from someone that I don't like or trust to begin with?"*

"Playing poker" is clearly not for everyone, but fortunately there is another mode of negotiation that provides a palatable alternative. I call this second style of negotiation, *"laying your cards on the table."* "Laying your cards on the table" involves openness, full-disclosure and trust. This is the opposite of "playing one's cards close to the vest," as is essential in a "poker game." When people "lay their cards on the table," there are no hidden agendas, strategic ploys or manipulations against an opponent. In fact, there is no opponent at all if the other party in the negotiation is willing to put her cards on the table as well so that the two participants can work together towards a mutually satisfying agreement.

"Laying my cards on the table" means that I will reveal exactly what I want and exactly what resources I have for getting it. In the car buying example, it means telling the salesperson up front what car I want and what price I am prepared to pay. When I "lay my cards on the table," I don't give an offer that is outrageously low, knowing that we will haggle to a more reasonable price. I don't threaten to go elsewhere as a means of leveraging. I don't ask for options that I don't really want, knowing I will use these to manipulate the final terms. Instead, I let my cards be seen in the full light for what they are so that the salesperson knows what I want and what I am prepared to do in order to obtain it.

> "I am going to be honest with you up front. I would really like the special edition Mustang and I can pay twenty-two thousand dollars cash, no financing, no trade-in. That is my absolute best offer. Take it or leave it."

"Laying your cards on the table" is very different from "playing poker," yet in our capitalistic society, both styles of negotiation have their place. My personal preference may be a "cards on the table" approach. However, if I am dealing with an opponent who insists on "playing poker," I may be putting myself into a position of extreme disadvantage by sticking to an open, revealing mode of dealing. Personally, I prefer operating with my "cards on the table" and I try to do so whenever it seems viable. However, I am prepared and willing to "play poker" if the situation calls for it. I, for one, do not want to expose my vulnerabilities and give away potential leverage when I am facing an opponent who is out to get the maximum he can extract from the deal. I would prefer to have us *both* put our "cards on the table," but if my opponent refuses to (even if he pretends to), I am reluctant to put myself in a position of weakness from which I may be taken advantage of.

It is usually not prudent to "lay your cards on the table" with an opponent who is set on "playing poker."

While "poker playing" is justifiable or even preferable in some arenas, there are certain types of relationships in which "poker playing" is an anathema. For instance, if my doctor, good friend or spouse is the one I am interacting with, I need to have "the cards on the table" if the relationship is to serve its intended purpose. In relationships built on trust, there is no room for the burdens of strategic plotting, potential deception or hidden agendas inherent in "poker playing."

In a marriage or a significant love relationship, where there are pre-existing expectations for openness, honesty and trust, negotiating with "cards on the table" is *essential.* In marriage, there is little if any room for "poker" since the goal of negotiation is not only to settle disparities, but also to promote further intimacy and trust in the process. As we have seen, "poker" pits **opponents** against one another while "laying cards on the table" allows for **partners** to work with each other towards a mutually satisfying end.

"Poker" creates *winners and losers* while "laying your cards on the table" promotes the best interests of both parties.

When partners are able and willing to "lay their cards on the table" with one another, there is a feeling of mutual concern, respect and optimism. Discrepancies and disagreements may still prove formidable and difficult to negotiate, but the elements of trust and teamwork go a long way in helping the process proceed smoothly. Partners feel that they are working together to achieve the common goal of mutual satisfaction, rather than haggling with one another over who will win and who will lose. To highlight the benefits of "laying cards on the table" as the preferable approach over "playing poker" in personal and other relationships, the following two examples contrast the styles and potential consequences of each method. First we will look at a "poker game" negotiation.

Ernie is a sales representative preparing to go on a business trip to Orlando, Florida. His wife, Beth, wanted to go with Ernie and bring the kids so that they could have a vacation together. Ernie, however, had his sights set on staying with two buddies after his convention and playing golf. He really didn't want to turn this trip into a family vacation. He knew, however, that Beth didn't like his two friends because they are both divorced, heavy drinkers and women-chasers. Ernie didn't need to drink or chase women, but he did want to get in a few days of golf. He decided to keep his real agenda hidden and to try to negotiate Beth out of her vacation plans.

"Honey, I just don't think this is a good time to try to pull off a vacation. The kids have school and soccer, and you've got your parents coming in two weeks."

Beth smiled and replied, "I know we can make it work. The kids can miss a few days of school and I won't have any trouble getting things set up for my parents before we leave for Florida. Come on, Ernie, the kids and I really need a family getaway. Besides, it'll be fun."

Ernie looked down and shook his head. "It's just not the right time, Beth. I'm going to be tied up in meetings the entire week. I'm not going to be able spend any time with you and the kids. It won't be a family vacation at all. I don't see how that will be any fun."

"You told me that the convention only lasted until Friday," Beth stated a bit miffed. "Besides, you are always telling me how boring these events are and how easy it is to sneak off and do your own thing."

"Well, this trip is different," Ernie argued. "My boss will be there the entire time and we have a series of meetings set up over the weekend to try and nail down several key accounts. It's just not going to work out."

Beth began to get more irritated. "Fine, then the kids I will just go and see Disneyworld by ourselves while you're off doing your important business. At least we'll get the benefit of your hotel room and we can spend whatever free time you are able to squeeze in with us."

Ernie searched his mind for alternatives and offered, "Look, why don't you and the kids fly out on Monday after I finish up everything. Then we can spend a few uninterrupted days together as a family."

Beth shook her head. "The following week won't work," she responded. "I've got to chair the PTA meeting and take my sister to the hospital for her surgery."

Ernie started to get exasperated. "Can't someone else chair that stupid meeting, and hasn't your sister ever heard of a taxi?"

"Where in the world are you coming from, Ernie? It sounds to me like you just don't want the kids and me to be with you at all."

Ernie calmed down and tried to backpedal. "Come on, Honey, it's not like that. I just don't think this is the right time or the right business trip to try and turn into a vacation. Look, I've got another conference in March down in San Diego. Why don't we try to plan something for the family then?"

Beth, still feeling hurt, suspicious and put off, held her ground. "You're still not hearing me, Ernie. The kids and I need a break now, not in March. I don't see how our presence is going to interfere with your business obligations. We'll just come and do our thing while you go off and do yours. Maybe it won't be a family vacation, but at least it will be a break for us."

Ernie knew at this juncture that Beth was set on going to Florida one way or the other. There seemed to be no talking her out of it. His golf plans were pretty much shot at this point and he figured that he might as well go ahead and turn the damned trip into a family vacation. Maybe that way he could still meet his buddies at a later time in San Diego.

"Okay, Beth," he conceded angrily. "You win. We'll all go to Orlando together. I'll see what I can do about getting some meetings rescheduled and we'll have your damned family vacation just the way you want. I certainly hope that will make you happy."

Beth stared at Ernie in dismay. "How is that supposed to make me happy, Ernie? You're acting like a spoiled little kid who isn't getting his way. I want us to go on a vacation where we can all be happy."

Ernie continued to sulk and fume. "Well, I'm sorry Beth. That's about the best I can do."

Ernie has chosen not to "lay his cards on the table;" so he proceeds to "play poker" with Beth. He works to manipulate her out of her desire for a family vacation so that he can achieve his goal of playing golf with his buddies. In this situation, Ernie already knows that Beth doesn't approve of his two friends and Ernie is certain that his desire to spend a few days with them will not hold up against Beth's more noble desire for some family time together. Ernie figures that if he really "put his cards on the table," he would not only lose his opportunity for golfing, but he would also have to endure yet another lecture from Beth about his poor choice of friends. In the end, however, Ernie is unable to argue Beth into submission, and so he finally folds and concedes the game. He declares Beth the winner and himself the loser. The real result, however, is that both partners lose. Both he and Beth end the process of negotiation with feelings of hurt, frustration and resentment.

For the sake of comparison, let's suppose Ernie and Beth addressed the same situation with a different negotiating approach, the approach of "laying cards on the table." It's not that the resolution of the problem will necessarily be any easier, but the process will have a much better chance of resulting in more positive feelings overall. The new conversation might go something like this:

"Ernie, the kids and I really want to go with you to Orlando."

Ernie looked up at his wife and responded, "I don't really want to turn this into a family vacation, Honey. I've got meetings to attend early in the week, and Jerry and Steve and I were planning to play golf together for a couple of days before I headed home."

Beth looked at Ernie with her eyebrows raised. "You never said anything about meeting up with those two."

"I know you hate them, but they happen to be friends of mine," Ernie replied. "I knew that if I told you I was going to go golfing with them, you would just give me a hard time about it."

Beth replied, "It's not the golfing that I mind. Those two lushes just have a reputation for being jerks and I don't have any respect or trust for either of them."

"So you're saying you don't trust me either?" Ernie blurted out defensively.

"I'm not saying that at all," Beth retorted. "Just because I don't like Jerry or Steve doesn't mean I don't trust you or that I mind you playing golf with them. I'll admit that I'd prefer you to keep better company, but I understand they're your friends." Beth saw a surprised look on Ernie's face and she continued, "But that's not the issue, Ernie. The issue is that the kids and I need a break and it would be really nice if we could use this trip as an opportunity to be together as a family."

Ernie listened intently and said, "I understand, Beth. It's just that I really had my heart set on a few days of golfing. I guess I've needed a break too, but a different kind than you have in mind."

Beth reached over and took Ernie's hand. "Is there any way you can set up another weekend for you and the guys to go somewhere and play golf? It would mean a lot to the kids and me. This is really the only week that will work for us in the near future. Would you please be willing to do this for us, Ernie?"

Ernie saw how important this vacation was to Beth and knew she was going to be very hurt and upset if he didn't agree to bring them all to Florida. He still didn't like having to change his plans and knew his buddies would give him a hard time, but Ernie felt accommodating his family was the right thing to do at this point.

"Okay, Beth," he conceded, "I'll make some calls and re-arrange my plans. I guess a family vacation would be good for us all. But I am going to hold you to your promise to let me schedule a golf weekend away with Steve and Jerry."

Beth hugged Ernie and gave him a big kiss. "It's a deal, Ernie. I can't tell you how happy this makes me and how excited the kids are going to be. Thank you, Honey. Thanks for being such a good sport."

The fact that Ernie was able to "lay his cards on the table" results in a much different outcome even though the family is still heading for Orlando. The "cards on the table" example is not devoid of conflict, but the partners now communicate in a way that clearly places them on the same side, working together toward a solution that meets both of their needs.

One element in reaching a workable solution is for each partner to honestly assess the level of importance that his or her individual desires hold. When a person can prioritize the differing values of his or her many needs, they can advocate these needs at a level commensurate with the genuine intensity of their wishes. Some things are more important than others and we need to attribute the appropriate value to each. For instance, playing golf is important to Ernie, but in the larger scheme of things *when* he plays is not crucial. However, on a relative scale, it does seem vital to Beth that this one chance for a family vacation is not lost. Ernie successfully perceives that Beth's issue has more weight for her than playing golf at a specific time holds for him. He is willing to look at the situation objectively and grant that Beth's strong desire outweighs his mild preference. By honestly assessing the value of their needs, Ernie lays the groundwork to get what he wants at a future time.

Each partner does concede something in the exchange—Ernie gives up his original golf plans and Beth will put up with Ernie going away later with two people she doesn't really like or trust. However, though neither partner wins, negotiation does seem to produce a feeling of "winning" for both partners. Beth gets her wish for a family vacation and Ernie will eventually have his weekend of golf. Most important, however, this conversation, unlike the previous "poker" negotiation, results in a shared sense of care, trust and relational affirmation. Ernie's and Beth's status as *true partners* is affirmed and upheld through their open and direct exchange. They have not only creatively settled their conflict over this particular trip, but have succeeded in strengthening their relationship in the process.

**Successful negotiations, where
partners "lay their cards on the table,"
not only resolve conflicts, but serve
to strengthen relational bonds.**

INTERNAL COMPROMISES

To negotiate with "cards on the table," partners must begin with a clear understanding and expression of their desired goals. Too often, we tend to anticipate what might be *doable* or *allowable* instead of beginning with an accurate representation of what it is that we genuinely want. We make assumptions, which may prove true or false, concerning what we perceive our partners will agree to or accept, and then we filter our communication to accommodate these perceptions. This **"internal compromise"** is commonly seen in the courtship phase of a relationship, when partners go out of their way to make a favorable impression. During dating, a person wants to be liked and accepted, and he or she therefore presents himself or herself in a manner that he or she *thinks* will be pleasing to the other. The dater tends to predict what the other person will like, value or appreciate and represent this as his own preference. The following situation is a good example of how this process of anticipation and accommodation can occur.

Kyle and Sylvia have been out together three times after being fixed-up by a mutual friend. They have really hit it off and both are hopeful that this might work out to be the "magic relationship" they have been looking for. The initial attractions, both physical and emotional, were strong. Sylvia was waiting for Kyle to call her up to set up their next big date. After waiting for what seemed like forever, the phone finally rang.

"Sylvia? Hi, this is Kyle. I hope I haven't caught you at a bad time."

Sylvia tried to get her heartbeat to slow down. "Not at all, Kyle, I've been hoping to hear from you."

Kyle, who had spent hours rehearsing for this call, proceeded with his well-thought-out script. "Well, I was wondering if you'd be free to go out to dinner tomorrow night?"

Sylvia bit her lip. She had her yoga class Thursday nights and never missed it for anything. She wished Kyle would have suggested Friday night instead, but didn't want to risk losing this chance to be together,

"Tomorrow night works great for me," she said cheerfully.

Kyle was elated and said, "I haven't made any reservations yet because I wanted to find out what kind of food you might be interested in."

Sylvia thought about her current Weight Watcher's diet but replied, "Oh, I'm really flexible. I like just about any kind of food. Where would you like to go?"

Kyle hesitated for a moment. He was really in the mood for Thai food, but that seemed like such a risk—he thought it might be too spicy or unusual for Sylvia. Besides, he thought he should take her some place really nice. Alfonso's was an elegant option, but for some reason, Kyle didn't think Sylvia would like Italian. Trying to impress her with his sophistication, the next words just seemed to jump out of his mouth, "How about Fleur de Lys?" Immediately Kyle realized that he hadn't asked the sixty-four dollar question—instead he had just asked the two hundred sixty-four dollar question.

Sylvia didn't know what to say. She loved going up to the city to dine, but had heard rumors of how expensive Fleur de Lys was. Rich French food would play havoc with her diet, but it sounded like this was really where Kyle wanted to take her. She ignored her hesitations and quickly responded, "That sounds perfect! I can hardly wait."

Kyle felt his heart sink a bit and his bank account drop a lot as he calmly said, "Great, then it's all set. I'll pick you up around six." He couldn't believe he had been so stupid. Not only was he going to drop a lot of money, but the truth was, he didn't even like French food.

"I'm so excited," Sylvia said, trying to smile but thinking wistfully of missing her yoga class and cheating on her diet. "I'll see you at six."

In fact, both Kyle and Sylvia have falsely portrayed themselves in an effort to win the affection of one another. Neither has acted out of any malicious intent, yet both have been dishonest and deceptive about their personal wants and preferences in an attempt to please their partners. The irony is that, in the end, *neither* Kyle nor Sylvia get what he or she wants. Their fear of disappointing the other and putting the relationship at risk results in a strategic negotiation which miserably fails. In this case, they are playing a distorted variation of "poker" in which each person tries to let the other win. The result, however, is a lose-lose conclusion that sets up the potential for resentment and severe misunderstanding.

> *Strategic* negotiations which are
> aimed at *letting the other person win* can
> easily backfire and result in more conflict.

Sylvia and Kyle are both driven by their infatuation and need to impress each other in hopes for a long-term relationship. Their motives are pure, but their communication is distorted. They do manage to avoid outward conflict and succeed in arranging another date together, but the costs of their deceptive negotiation will most likely come back to haunt them. Kyle has led Sylvia to believe that he enjoys French food and doesn't mind paying a high price for it—neither of which is true. Sylvia, on the other hand, has not been open or honest with Kyle about the importance of her yoga class, the sacrifice she made to miss it, her current diet, and her uneasiness about the cost of their upcoming meal. We can almost predict the fallout that might ensue as their poor communication turns to misunderstanding and eventually to confusion and upset:

- *"I thought you loved French cuisine."*

- *"I never knew you were on a diet."*

- *"How was I supposed to know that your yoga class was so important; you didn't seem to mind missing it last month."*

- *"How dare you accuse me of being an 'expensive date' when you're the one who picked that outrageous restaurant to begin with."*

- *"For God's sake, why didn't you say something in the first place?"*

We shouldn't be too hard on Kyle and Sylvia. After all, they *are* blinded by their need to be loved. However, this pattern of anticipation and "internal compromise" is not restricted to those entranced by the infatuation of a new relationship. Couples who have been together for decades frequently enter negotiations with false or distorted proposals. Long-time partners may feel that they know their spouse so well that there is no need to ask directly for the others' opinions or preferences. Instead, the knowing partner uses his own assumptions to negotiate the exchange in his own mind with the intention of delivering an acceptable proposal. A glimpse into the mind of Floyd preparing to take his wife Emma to the movies illustrates this point quite clearly.

"I know if I tell Emma I want to go to the theater to see the Eastwood western, *A Fistful of Dollars,* she will say no and launch into a lecture about how perverted I am for liking such 'trash'. On the other hand, if I ask her what movie she wants to see, she's going want to go to that artsy-fartsy theater across town and see whatever weird foreign movie their showing. I don't think I could hold down my Junior Mints if I had to sit through that again. Maybe I should just ask her to go see the new Jim Carrey film. We both like comedies and I'm sure she'll go for that. I hate to give up on Clint Eastwood tonight, but Jim Carrey is probably the best I can do."

Floyd is operating on the assumption that Emma would be unwilling to see the action western he prefers. He may be right—after all, he and Emma have been together for many years and know each other pretty well. Or do they? Most long-term partners believe they intimately understand each other, but it is astonishing how frequently I see couples in therapy where one or both partners feel that the other person really doesn't know him or her at all. So often I hear comments such as:

- *"He thinks he knows what I like, but he hasn't got a clue."*

- *"I wish, for just once, she would ask me first before assuming what I want."*

- *"You'd think that after twenty-five years together he would get it right by now."*

- *"I swear I've told her a million times, but she still doesn't seem to understand."*

The length of a relationship is not necessarily correlated with how well people really know each other. Some twenty-five-year relationships that have stagnated are really one-year relationships repeated twenty-five times. The keys to growth and in-depth understanding are openness and attention, not time.

**Emotional intimacy is not
simply a function of time.**

Many misperceptions and distorted assumptions seem to be tied to the phenomenon of "internal compromise"—where partners misrepresent their own authentic feelings and anticipate the responses of their mates in an effort to avoid conflict and potential criticism. Instead of negotiating with their partner, they negotiate in their own minds and then go on to deliver a filtered and "internally compromised" offer. Floyd, in the previous example, will most likely end up saying something like, "Emma, dear, how would you like to go and see the new Jim Carrey movie tonight down at the Starlight Theater?"

But let's suppose that Emma doesn't want to see the Jim Carrey movie and suggests something entirely different. The conversation could easily escalate to something like the following.

"Floyd, I'd love to go the movies tonight, but I'd much rather go see *Moonlight in Venice*."

Floyd responds with irritation in his voice, "What's wrong with the Jim Carrey movie?"

"I can't stand Jim Carrey," Emma retorts.

"I thought you liked him."

"I hate him," Emma replies, "Besides, I'm in the mood for something more romantic."

"I thought you enjoyed going to see comedies," Floyd protests. "Damn it, Emma, I've already ruled out the movie I really want to go to. Why do we always have to see the movie you choose?"

"What did you want to go see, Floyd?" Emma asks a bit confused by his level of frustration.

"Oh, never mind," Floyd bellows. "Let's just stay home and watch television. I don't know why I ever invite you to do things in the first place."

Emma may feel blindsided at this point. She has no idea that Floyd has already made a compromise in his mind prior to their conversation. Floyd feels unappreciated and unacknowledged, because he has already made an accommodation to meet Emma on what he perceives are her own terms, but Emma has no way of knowing this. All she can see is a selfish, angry, stubborn man who quits when he doesn't get his own way. Both partners leave this exchange angry and disappointed. Their evening is pretty much ruined. Worse than anything else, each partner goes away feeling misunderstood and unfairly treated. Floyd's internal negotiation, which was conducted as a means of *avoiding conflict*, has resulted in far more friction and antagonism than he ever imagined.

Unilateral "internal compromises" are usually performed as a means of *conflict avoidance*, yet they often result in bigger conflicts than they prevent.

Real intimacy involves being in touch with your emotions and needs and expressing them openly to your partner. It means fully being yourself and allowing your partner to experience the authentic person that you are. People often think of intimacy only in sexual terms, but the physical expression of yourself through sex is only one facet of intimacy. For someone like Floyd, relational intimacy starts with telling Emma from the outset what movie he really wants to see. When Floyd reveals to Emma that he wants to go to *A Fistful of Dollars*, he is exposing a small part of his true self. Whether or not the couple ends up seeing this film is far less important than Floyd's capacity to be himself and to express himself in the relationship. If Floyd felt that it was truly safe, and if he were fully willing to "lay all of his cards on the table," then he might approach Emma by saying:

> "Emma, I really want to go to the movies tonight and I really would like to see *A Fistful of Dollars*. We don't have to see that particular film, but it is the one I want to go to the most."

Being this direct and open leaves Floyd vulnerable to both criticism and rejection. Emma might ridicule him for his bad taste in movies and she can refuse to go see the film he has chosen. However, if Floyd does take the risk of communicating directly—"laying all of his cards on the table"—he will increase the intimacy of the relationship and he also will at least create the possibility of getting what he truly wants. Who knows, perhaps Emma will be willing to try the Eastwood film, or perhaps she is willing to trade this choice for her choice of movies next week, or maybe she just wants to spend the time with Floyd, or . . . The fact is, there are countless reasons why Emma might agree, all of which Floyd has overruled by assuming she would *never* want to go.

The most prevalent reason partners resist being direct with each other involves their perceived sense of safety. None of us want to be rejected or put down, yet this is exactly what we risk if we choose to express ourselves openly. In order for me to be willing to expose my uncensored preferences and needs, I need to have confidence in the following three things:

1) My relationship has room for me to be *different* than my mate.

2) My partner will *respect* my opinions, feelings and needs even if she strongly disagrees with them. (She will not ridicule or dogmatically lecture me about "being wrong.")

3) My partner will *care* about how I feel and *take my needs into consideration* when we approach the task of negotiating an agreement.

When these three factors exist, partners can feel safe and confident in expressing themselves fully and true intimacy can burgeon. People can lay all of their cards on the table and know that, even though they might not get exactly what they want, they consistently have the freedom to earnestly declare their desires and have their wishes honored and carefully considered by their partner. In the safety and security of a loving, intimate, respectful union, partners can fully be themselves and work toward agreements where the needs of both parties are validated and upheld.

When I trust that I am operating in an atmosphere of freedom and security, I can begin any negotiation with a clear and accurate disclosure of my wants. I will not *insist* on always having to get my way, but I will see the importance of expressing myself as both an intimate revelation of my personhood and as the legitimate starting point of any negotiation with my spouse. I will try my best to resist the impulses to make assumptions about my partner's feelings, to pre-negotiate compromises in my own mind, or to overrule any option without "checking it out" first. To put it simply, I will allow *my partner* to be the author, authority and advocate for her own feelings. I will let her be *responsible* for articulating her own needs so that I can both consider them in our negotiation and, more importantly, come to *know her more fully* as a means of expanding our intimacy.

CONCLUSION

Though couples frequently define "a lack of communication" as the core problem of their relationship, non-communication should be viewed as a relational defense mechanism that serves to protect the partners and the relationship from unexpressed conflicts. Working to improve communication in a manner that allows partners to voice their true feelings and needs results in the emergence of discrepancies, disagreements and potential disputes. Couples must be equipped to face the challenge of working through conflict if they are to accept the risks of open communication. Partners need to feel secure and confident that the love, trust and commitment of their relationships can weather the storms of negotiating differences.

Couples must observe and choose whether they want to relate as either **partners** or **opponents**. Partners work together as a team to find win-win solutions to the conflicts of their expectations, values and needs. Opponents, on the other hand, battle one another in an attempt to promote their individual interests and desires. Partners relate with feelings of mutual trust, devotion and optimism. Opponents operate with a sense of suspicion, selfishness, and competition.

The challenge for couples is to learn how to remain *partners* when relational conflicts push them toward being opponents.

We have looked at two basic modes of negotiation: "playing poker," and "laying cards on the table." When people negotiate in the "poker" style, they take a strategic, manipulative and even deceptive approach with the sole aim of defeating the opposition. They view the other negotiating party as their opponent and work against their adversary in the most powerful and effective ways they can. In "poker," the unilateral goal is always to win.

The second approach to negotiating, "laying cards on the table," allows individuals to operate in an open and trusting manner. Instead of being opponents, people who "lay their cards on the table" seek to unite as teammates in an effort to attain resolutions that preserve the interests of both parties. The goal is to work together to create a situation where everybody wins.

Finally, we have examined the phenomenon of "internal compromise"—a process where one partner attempts to predict the responses of his mate and modify his own requests accordingly. Individuals perform internal compromises as a method of self-protection (not being criticized or ridiculed) and as a means of avoiding potential conflict. Internal compromises are really another variation of "playing poker," and as such, usually serve to create more opposition and fallout than they ever prevent.

It is clear that significant and meaningful love relationships require a "cards on the table" approach. Since the goal of couples is not only to settle differences but also to consistently affirm love and trust in the relationship, there is really no room for "poker" in love relationships. Couples must elevate their role as partners and remain committed to working as a team. In the safety and security of this higher form of union, differences and disputes can be addressed and resolved openly, and the relationship can continue to grow, mature and flourish.

Chapter 8

DEBT FORGIVENESS
Wiping the Slate Clean

Forgive us our debts as we forgive our debtors.
- The Lord's Prayer

We have already explored how emotional debts can be settled through the use of specific and mutually acceptable forms of compensation. While tangible payment is always one possible avenue of debt resolution, there is another passageway to relationship satisfaction which offers the prospect of full settlement without the necessity of any actual exchange. Through a free and active choice to unilaterally discharge debts, partners who are relationship creditors have the option and the capacity to extend *forgiveness*, thereby entirely wiping the slate clean for both the debtor and themselves.

Debt forgiveness brings about full resolution for both parties through one powerful act.

In the realm of international economics, the forgiving of financial debts encompasses a spectrum of complex global situations. Debtor countries owing billions of dollars to creditor nations as a result of commercial trade, general aid or war reparations may eventually ask that their debts be forgiven. The creditor nation can choose to discharge all rightful claims to payment in a unilateral act of exoneration arising from economic imperatives, political purposes or a strategic act of goodwill.

On a more personal scale, private loans from one individual to another may be canceled as an act of kindness or generosity—the money mom and dad advanced toward a car down payment may eventually transform into a gift, or the twenty bucks your buddy loaned you in a pinch may later be shrugged off as a token of friendship. Regardless of the nature of the relationship or the magnitude of the debt, forgiveness always stands as a reasonable, acceptable and legitimate form of monetary debt release.

The dismissal of a *financial* debt usually stems from a rational economic analysis and represents some degree of benevolence on the part of the creditor. But when we turn from economics and enter the province of human relationships, the granting of forgiveness embodies a truly transforming and gracious act of a magnitude far beyond any financial decision. Whereas the entitlement to recompense is the right of any legitimate emotional creditor, the capacity and willingness to forgive transcend the demands of justice and exalt the virtue of generosity. While *collecting* rightful compensation may require dull persistence and a dose of patience, it certainly does not demand anything that resembles kindness or forbearance. Relational *forgiveness*, on the other hand, is a self-affirming experience which evolves from empathy, compassion and gentleness within the human spirit.

THE BASIS FOR HUMAN FORGIVENESS

All human beings are imperfect creatures, and interactions between us are thus riddled with imperfection. Relationships are constantly punctured by mistakes, insensitivity, cruelties and a myriad of personal violations. In human relationships, it is not a question of whether such breaches will take place, but rather how these emotional fissures will be dealt with when they inevitably occur. The motivation to restore shattered ties and to actively seek reconciliation with our partner is a regenerative process which has its origins in the human conscience.

Our conscience provides the unique ability to morally reflect on our actions and their consequences and then to willfully re-direct our behavior based on mindful decision-making. Conscience is a product of both our awareness (consciousness) and our ethical drive (conscientiousness). It is what enables us to determine right from wrong and to purposefully set a more positive course of action. Some would argue that our moral capacity is what separates us from the lower animals—our ability to make judgments and to intentionally alter our behavior rather than instinctively playing out an imprinted pattern of response.

Conscience is the uniquely human attribute that sets us apart as responsible agents, fully accountable for the decisions we make and the actions we choose.

The nature of our conscience allows for two key responses to any relational transgression:

1) *Repentance* by the perpetrator who committed the violation; and

2) *Forgiveness* by the person who has been violated.

Both of these concepts are worth a closer look.

Repentance

Repentance is the admission of personal wrong-doing and the willingness to re-direct our behavior along a more positive course. The prerequisite for repentance is the conscious awareness of truly blameworthy conduct—there can be no contrition without the admission of culpability.

The seed of repentance germinates from an inner voice which beckons us to acknowledge our personal mistakes and offenses. As we admit to our transgressions, the conviction grows to modify our behavior and alter our path as a means of rectifying errors. A decision to repent always springs from a sober contemplation of our behavior and its ensuing consequences. Repentance manifests in our intentional movement toward positive change—it elevates the human experience to a moral plane above animalistic drive and primitive instinct.

Forgiveness

The same moral capacity which fosters repentance also spawns the possibility of forgiveness—the compassionate act of relinquishing our claim to restitution for the transgressions and harm which others have inflicted on us. Whereas repentance is the act of willful *self-change* based on our own wrong-doings, forgiveness is always *outwardly directed* toward those who have trespassed against us. Forgiveness thus becomes the connective force of our conscience to our external human relationships.

The depth and complexity of forgiveness emerges when we look at the five definitive qualities which constitute its nature.

1. Forgiveness is exclusive to *human* relationships.

Forgiveness is only possible in a world that includes intentionality and purposeful behavior, traits solely attributable to human beings. We do not think in terms of forgiving a tree for growing in the wrong spot, since we do not attribute conscious choice or moral accountability to a tree. In the same vein, we have no need to forgive a mountain lion for killing a deer, since the lion is simply seen as fulfilling its instinctual drive for survival.

When it comes to our fellow human beings, however, we do make the assumption of some degree of willful, deliberate behavior, and, therefore, we hold one another responsible for our actions. The level of accountability is a function of many variables—age, mental capacity, emotional state and the specific circumstances of the situation. For instance, we would never attribute the same level of responsibility to a two-year-old autistic child for hitting her mother as we would to the same act carried out by a normal eighteen-year-old. Accountability does vary in degree, but the fact remains, once some level of personal moral responsibility has been determined, we are justified in holding one another accountable.

Because forgiveness is rooted in human consciousness and accountability, it is an act which functions exclusively in the realm of human beings. Forgiveness is a meaningless concept apart from human relationships.

2. Only those who have directly suffered an injustice can forgive.

In the same way that repentance requires an acceptance of blame, forgiveness can only emanate from an individual who has sustained substantive harm or injustice. Furthermore, it is only the injured party who has the right to forgive. I may be angry or feel vindictive over the genocide of the Jews, the assassination of John F. Kennedy or the abduction of a young child, but unless I am a direct victim of these injustices, I have no platform from which to forgive. Forgiveness is only valid when it is granted by a person who has both the position and the right to forgive.

3. Forgiveness is an alternative to justice.

The concept of justice is founded on the principle of sufficient payment for wrongful deeds. We may argue over what constitutes fair punishment (an eye for an eye, a slap on the wrist for stealing candy, five million dollars for a malpractice suit, castration for the violent rapist), but the balancing of reasonable consequences against injurious actions is always the sole concern of justice.

On the other hand, the act of forgiveness constitutes the opposite response to the application of justice. Although forgiveness also begins with the recognition that an injustice has taken place in which real blame can be attributed, the person who chooses to forgive elects freely to set aside his right to restitution. Instead, the forgiver willfully chooses to fully exonerate the blameworthy party in the total absence of any compensation—there is no tangible balancing involved. Forgiveness is thus a singular act which wipes the slate completely clean once and for all, eliminating any pursuit of just retribution.

4. Forgiveness is for the benefit of the forgiver, not just the forgiven.

While any individual who is forgiven obviously benefits from the release of her obligation to repay, there is clearly a substantial gain for the forgiver as well. The person electing forgiveness is not only freed from the onerous task of extracting payment but also sheds the emotional burdens attached to the insistent pursuit of justice. As long as recompense is expected and sought, the violated party has a tendency to stew in the juices of her own righteous indignation. The offended person is mired in feelings ranging from simmering resentment to boiling vengefulness as he broods over the injustice he has suffered and is haunted by his lust for retribution.

But the gracious act of forgiveness has a self-healing quality which works deep within the heart of the forgiver. While it is rarely an instantaneous transformation, the progressive and palliative cleansing enables the forgiver to achieve a higher state of inner peace and reconciliation. The forgiver does absolve the offender, but more importantly he liberates himself. And because forgiveness not only erases the emotional debt but also dissolves the bitterness and rancor in the heart of the forgiver, it is an act which ultimately benefits the giver far more than the receiver.

5. Forgiving does not require forgetting.
The experience of forgiveness is very different for the forgiver than it is the forgiven. From the perspective of the person who *receives* forgiveness, the act of forgiving always occurs in a circumscribed moment of time. Once forgiveness has been granted, the violator is fully acquitted and no basis exists for any ongoing demands of restitution. Discharge of emotional debt means totally expunging the debt—the act of forgiveness serves as a "once and for all" offering which cannot be revoked. As far as the violator is concerned, the offense has been forgiven and forgotten.

But for the forgiver, the act of forgiving is more of a developing process than a singular event in time. Because residual resentments may persist, the forgiver may indeed harbor a certain amount of ongoing memory and emotional attachment to the offense, even after forgiveness has been granted. The popular notion that "to forgive is to forget" may indeed be the noble ideal. The realities of the human heart and the imperfections of our nature do not always allow for perfect forgiveness. We may still choose to forgive even though we may not quickly or ever forget.

THREE PHASES OF FORGIVING
The subjective experience of forgiving can vary dramatically from one person to another due to the personality and temperament of the individual. For some, forgiveness comes easily—almost like a natural current within their spirit. But for others, forgiveness requires mindful determination, dedication and

even fortitude. The subjective experiences of forgiving can best be understood by a consideration of the three sequential phases which constitute the act.

Phase I. Relinquishing Our Resentment

The first phase of forgiving involves a movement within the forgiver from intense, grinding resentment toward a reduced level of emotionality. The initial resentment which accompanies any injustice must sufficiently dissipate to a level that allows the injured party to begin letting go. There is no necessity for total emotional resolution before the act of forgiveness can take place. But the pain and enmity must subside to a level which permits the forgiver to relinquish their grip on the need for reprisal.

For some people, the experience of releasing their bitterness and desire for revenge seems to flow naturally, as though they were endowed with emotional glands which spontaneously secrete compassion and forbearance. These fortunate individuals tend to experience forgiveness as an unforced surrendering of animosity which springs from a gracious heart. But most of us find it far more difficult to let go of our pain and rancor. We are prone to brooding righteously, churning in our lust for retribution and bearing our vexatious grudges into future days or even decades. For most people, emotions of kindness and leniency do not freely flow forth, and so we must actively wrestle with our bitterness rather than hoping it will somehow dissolve away all on its own.

The case of Joe and his father provides an apt example of an injured party struggling to forgive.

> Joe is a twenty-eight-year-old electrician who sought counseling after he learned that his father had been diagnosed with terminal lung cancer. Joe had not seen or spoken to his father in over eleven years. His father was an ex-marine captain whose overbearing manner and relentless criticisms drove Joe to leave home before finishing high school. In his father's eyes, Joe could never do anything right and would certainly never live up to his rigid standards. Their conflict was so acerbic that their final confrontation ended in a bloody fist fight.

When Joe fled from home to move to California, he made a decision to never speak to his father again. During his initial counseling session, Joe described his feelings, past and present.

"For all these years," he said, "any thoughts of my father ate away at my gut. I actually got an ulcer at one point, and I'm convinced he was the reason. I just couldn't get away from it—I hated him so much that I actually would lie in bed at night fantasizing about ways to get back at him. As the years went by, there were a few times when I considered calling him. But then I would remember why I needed to get away from him in the first place. Besides, why should it fall on my shoulders to have to initiate anything? He knows how to use a phone, for God's sakes. That's a big part of it—the man has never admitted he was wrong or said he was sorry about anything in his life. He can sure dish out blame to everyone else, but he could never own up to his screw-ups.

"Then I got the call from my mom about his cancer, and everything got confused. I could just picture the old, tough guy lying there in bed, helpless and weak. I know how much that has got to be tearing him apart. For the first time I felt my anger give way to pity. The reality of his dying has really gotten to me.

"I never expected to feel like this—it's almost like my hatred got short-circuited. My need to even the score doesn't seem so important now. I guess I've got to decide whether to try to forgive him for all the crap he heaped on me over the years, or whether to hold my ground and be willing to let him die without ever making up with him. I know I can't kid myself about this—I've got to live with my decision either way."

In situations such as Joe's, where pain and indignation are entrenched, prolonged resentment can continue until a shattering event breaks the hold of bitterness. Until the intensity of the caustic emotions sufficiently recedes, forgiveness can never be a possibility.

The offended party must guard against prematurely offering forgiveness—until the emotional fervor abates, impulsive attempts to forgive will always prove unstable and, in the end, will never last. All successful forgivers must be reconciled with their own feelings and must count the cost of what extending forgiveness will entail. Otherwise, bitter hostility may well up again and re-trigger toxic attitudes which belie the attempted act of forgiveness and ultimately prove it to be no forgiveness at all.

Phase II. Granting Forgiveness

Any decision to forgive another person always comes down to a willful determination. Because our emotions may not be fully aligned with our decision to forgive, we often elect forgiveness in the face of some residual hard feelings. In the moment we extend forgiveness, we may still bear remnants of unresolved hurt and resentment. But our resolve to relinquish our claim to restitution can override these impulses and enable us to pursue a path of pardon.

The case of Sheila and her husband Richard shows how a person can still extend forgiveness, even in the face of some ongoing hurt and hostility.

Sheila discovered three months ago that her husband Richard was having an affair with his secretary. After confronting him with the truth, Richard agreed to end the affair and transfer to a different branch office.

Sheila considered a divorce or a separation after she first learned about his unfaithfulness. She had always promised herself that she would never remain in a relationship with anyone she felt she couldn't trust, and this was certainly the worst betrayal she had ever gone through.

After months of hurting and obsessing angrily over the affair, Sheila's wrath diminished to the point where she could begin to put things into perspective. After weighing all of the options, Sheila came to realize that she still loved Richard and wanted to work toward restoring their marriage. Forgiving Richard was the essential step for moving forward.

"Richard," Sheila began, "I've thought things through and have come to the decision that I want to forgive you. What you did hurt me deeply and I've never been angrier about anything in my life. But I realize that I need to let go of my resentment if we are ever going to repair things between us. Don't get me wrong; I think what you did was horrible and self-ish—I don't see any excuse for it—but I realize that I need to forgive you and move on. I think it's the only way to preserve our marriage.

"You know me really well, Richard. You know I'm not the kind of person who easily forgives or forgets. That's just the way I am. So, I can't promise that I will never think about the affair again or feel upset about it in the future. What I can promise is that I forgive you and that I will never throw it up in your face again. Any left-over anger will be mine to sort out. As for us, I just want to focus on putting away the past and getting on with our lives together."

Sheila's ability to choose a course of behavior that runs counter to the tide of her emotion enables her to forgive even though she might not be able to excise the incident completely from her mind and heart. Ultimately, the restorative power of forgiveness combined with the healing force of time might even yield something that resembles a full amnesia to the betrayal she has suffered. However, humanity is more prone to residual echoes of both memory and emotion. Because of our imperfect nature, forgiveness often resembles a long-term commitment more than a spontaneous act of magic in which all is forgotten and all negative feelings evaporate. Banishing all bitterness and erasing the incident from memory are noble goals for all forgivers, but they are neither a requisite nor a realistic standard to impose.

Phase III. Coping With Lingering Resentment

Once forgiveness has been granted, the *forgiven* is liberated from any burden of repayment—he is free to resume life as though nothing ever happened. However, for the *forgiver*, there may still be an ongoing battle against vengeful emotions toward the offense and the offender.

While forgiveness requires a substantial dissipation of initial pain and hostility, some level of agitation will tend to persist. Even after emotions subside to a level which allows for authentic forgiveness to be granted, continued twinges of resentment can re-surface. The final phase of forgiveness is marked by the forgiver's continued efforts at coping with any residual emotions linked to the initial violation.

In some instances, this final phase is short-lived, for the forgiver may quickly experience a release from any lingering harsh feelings. In most cases, the process of contending with remnant thoughts and resentments is an unavoidable reality. In fact, dealing with the vestiges of bitter emotions may continue throughout life, depending on the temperament of the forgiver and the nature of the transgression involved.

The case of Barry and his brother Jay illustrates how a sincere forgiver must at times battle his own memories and impulses long after forgiveness has been granted.

When Barry was thirteen years old, his fifteen-year-old brother Jay was teasing him with their father's target pistol. The gun went off accidentally and Barry suffered a facial wound which left him disfigured and blind in his left eye.

Barry spoke of his ordeal twenty years later during a therapy session. "After the accident, I was in shock. I remained in critical care for the first week and then was in and out of hospitals over the next six months. Once they knew they couldn't save my eye, I still had to undergo three plastic surgeries. It was a horrible ordeal for any teenager.

"I knew Jay felt worse than anyone. Mom and Dad didn't try to punish him, because they knew how devastated he was. His punishment was having to watch me go through the years of treatments, knowing he was fully responsible for what had happened.

"It took me about three years, but I remember coming home from my final surgery and feeling like the worst was finally over. I went up to Jay's room and told him that I forgave him. He broke into tears and kept telling me how sorry he was and how he would do anything in the world to make things up to me. I just hugged him and told him that nothing was ever going to change what had happened, and that we both needed to put it to rest. That was really an important day for both of us, because I truly wanted to leave my anger behind, and Jay could tell that I was serious about forgiving him.

"Well, I have to admit, there are moments when the pain of the accident still comes back to haunt me. Sometimes it's actual physical pain in my facial nerves or the limitations of my depth perception. It's everything from having to give up certain sports to contending with the stares people give me in public. I know you're supposed to forgive and forget, but for me, the reminders are constantly there.

"It's hard not to fantasize about what my life would have been like if Jay had never taken out the gun. It's a struggle not to feel the resentment well up inside. But that has never changed my resolve to forgive Jay. The older I get, the happier I am to have him as my brother. But I don't think I'll ever forget what happened or totally get over my feelings. I guess that's just part of the baggage that comes with the situation."

For Barry, the final stage of living out forgiveness in the face of the piercing reminders of his trauma seems a never-ending struggle. The fact that Barry has to contend with lingering resentments in no way diminishes or nullifies his forgiveness. Barry's commitment to forgive requires that he cope with his own limitations and hardships without re-channeling blame toward his brother for the initial tragedy. The daily reminders of disfigurement and disability make his commitment to forgive a difficult one, but Barry has come to understand that the road of forgiveness is ultimately the best avenue for both his brother and himself.

As Barry continues to deal with the remnant thoughts and feelings which are an inevitable part of his daily life, he admirably fulfills his pledge of forgiveness by continuing his dedication to a self-determined course of letting go and moving ahead. Though some might argue Barry has not truly forgiven due to his inability to *forget*, in actuality, his perseverance and resolve demonstrate perhaps the highest form of a forgiving spirit—a spirit which stays its course in the face of bitter reminders.

> **Forgiveness is easy if memory of the violation fades, but it takes a dedicated soul to persist in the face of haunting echoes of the past.**

FORGIVING UNACKNOWLEDGED DEBTS

A final question which must be addressed is whether a debt must be acknowledged by the debtor before it can be forgiven by the creditor. There are many situations in which aggrieved creditors feel that something is owed to them, but the perceived debtor refuses to accept any responsibility. Debtors who perceive themselves as blameless may assert:

- *"I don't see that I did anything wrong."*

- *"I disagree that I owe you something."*

- *"I feel no need to apologize."*

- *"It's your issue, not mine—why are you blaming me?"*

In such instances, the creditors must decide whether they are able and willing to forgive the person who does not perceive that he was the cause of any infraction in the first place.

> **It is one thing to forgive someone who is remorseful and repentant, but it is quite another to forgive someone who admits to no wrong.**

In reality, it is possible for the creditor to forgive the offending party unilaterally. In fact, in situations which involve disavowal by an offender, forgiveness may be the only possible path to resolution since the denying debtor will never proffer payment. However, forgiving the unrepentant is a bitter pill to swallow, since it requires not only forgiving the original violation but also overlooking the debtor's blindness or refusal to accept any responsibility. Since acknowledgment of the debt is absent, there will be no recognition of the forgiveness, either. Creditors must be content with their own sense of internal resolution. This peace of mind, in the end, not only creates the healing force which comes from letting go, but also embodies the highest aspiration of a forgiving heart.

CONCLUSION

The settling of emotional debts is essential to the restoration and preservation of all healthy relationships. While there are numerous pragmatic ways of resolving relational debts, the kindhearted act of forgiveness is a unique extension of human compassion which not only liberates the debtor but also heals the heart of the creditor. Forgiveness soothes the soul and affirms the highest virtues of the human spirit.

The very nature of forgiveness allows for simultaneously setting relationships right on the day-to-day plane while also establishing a fresh, new starting place from which relationships can aspire to new levels of trust and love. Whenever creditors actively choose to settle debts by offering forgiveness rather than seeking restitution, it becomes a choice not simply for canceling the debt but ultimately for inspiring the whole relationship toward new dimensions of gracious caring. The intangible forces of love which surround forgiveness, therefore, render it the highest expression and most redemptive form of debt resolution.

Chapter 9

ESCAPING DEBTS
Termination Without Payment or Forgiveness

The candles burn their sockets,
The blinds let through the day,
The young man feels his pockets
And wonders what to pay.
- Alfred Edward Housman

Imagine that you borrowed a large sum of money to invest in your rapidly expanding business. You willingly take on the risk of such an enormous debt burden, because the business has all indications of being a huge success. But overnight, disaster strikes. Your life-long friend and business partner disappears into thin air with the company's plane, the company's secretary and the company's entire bank account. You wake up the next morning with no assets or resources but with the continuing responsibility for repaying the now unpayable debt. What would you do?

Just as in financial obligations, emotional debts have the same potential for hitting a brick wall of hopelessness and reaching a point of being irreconcilable. In such circumstances, depleted debtors may opt to escape their relational debts without the exchange of payment or the granting of forgiveness by the creditor. Although the feelings of satisfaction which come from settlement and resolution are absent when indebtedness is circumvented, there are indeed situations which make evasion of debt a viable route. Three ways of escaping emotional debts can be identified.

EMOTIONAL BANKRUPTCY – THE INABILITY TO PAY

Creditors in the financial world always risk the possibility that debtors will lose the means for ever paying back their debts. Whether it is due to a major corporation sinking under the weight of monstrous bank loans or an individual who is laid-off and cannot pay her mortgage, the holders of credit must sometimes face the circumstances in which debtors simply are unable to pay. In these instances, insolvent debtors are forced to take the desperate step of declaring bankruptcy, thus rendering their debt uncollectible. The filing of chapter 7 provides the destitute debtor with the opportunity for a "fresh start," even though the rightful creditor is left without restitution of any kind. In such circumstances, creditors have no choice but to accept their losses and write them off. In spite of their original agreements with creditors, bankrupt borrowers end up paying nothing and owing nothing.

Similarly, when *emotional* debts become too much to bear, one person in a relationship may see no realistic means for satisfying his relational creditor. The emotional debtor may be incapable of paying what is demanded or may decide that the price for settling a debt is simply too high. At this point, the debtor may declare emotional bankruptcy, proclaiming that he has neither the means nor desire to repay the existing debt. The exasperated creditor may refuse to relinquish her claim for payment—she may become irate and retaliatory—but ultimately, the creditor has no effective or satisfactory recourse against a debtor who refuses to pay. The disgruntled creditor can persist in frustrating attempts to extract payment, but it is clearly within the power of any debtor to remain in default.

The case of Paul and Leslie demonstrates how a relational debt can lead to emotional bankruptcy.

> Paul was a skilled amateur musician whose true passion in life was performing in jazz groups. Every chance he got—sometimes as often as four nights a week—Paul would be out until one o'clock in the morning either playing with his own band or sitting in on jam sessions. Early in their marriage, Leslie accompanied him frequently to the clubs and bars where he played. But she grew weary of the late hours and lost interest in the whole jazz scene. Although she frequently felt abandoned, Leslie tolerated Paul's

absences until his neglect went way over the line.

She described the traumatic incident that made her draw the line. "I was eight and a half months pregnant when Paul got a call to fill in for a sax player at a famous club in New Orleans. The gig would last four days and I begged him not to go. The doctor told me that I might deliver early and I desperately wanted him to be with me for the birth of our first child. He promised me that everything would work out and that he just couldn't pass up the opportunity to play with this hot group in New Orleans. So off he went over my repeated pleas for him to stay home.

"You can pretty much figure the rest. The night after he left, I went into sudden labor and had to call an ambulance to get to the hospital. There was no way I could reach Paul. I was rushed into the delivery room and required a C-section when they realized there was a problem with the baby's heartbeat. I've never felt so alone and scared in my life.

"My family finally reached Paul the next day and he got on the next flight home. He did come back, but I always felt he did so reluctantly. By then it didn't matter, anyway. I was so angry and hurt at his thoughtlessness for leaving me in the first place that I didn't really know if I ever wanted to see him again."

Paul picked up the story from here and said, "At first, she wouldn't even talk to me. I knew I had made a terrible mistake, but I wasn't sure what it would take to patch things up. I took some time off work to be home and help with the baby, but Leslie was still fuming. Finally I asked her what it was going to take to set things right. I had a sinking feeling what she would say.

"Just as I figured, Leslie demanded that I give up my music and start staying home like any responsible father should. I tried to talk her down, but she wouldn't budge. The way she saw it, it was either our marriage or my music.

"So, what could I do? For the next few weeks I canceled all my gigs and stayed home every night. But I was dying inside—music is such a part of me it was like cutting out my soul. It didn't take me long to realize that there was just no way I could deliver what she wanted. I couldn't stop being who I am just to make up for one really bad decision. That night I sat down with Leslie and laid it on the line.

"I told her that I was really sorry for leaving her when I did, but there was no way I could pay her price. I was willing to try and cut back, but I didn't have it in me to totally give up music. If she decided to kick me out, that would be up to her. However, I intended to keep on playing either way. There was really nothing else I could do."

Leslie's demand for restitution proved too high for Paul to meet. He neither wanted to nor felt he could set aside his music as a means of compensating his angry wife for the infraction he committed. For Paul, cutting out his music was like cutting out his heart. He came to realize that declaring emotional bankruptcy was his only real option. His passion for music was utterly incompatible with Leslie's demand for him to stay home every night. Now it will be up to Leslie, the unpaid creditor, to determine her response—she will either learn to live with Paul's refusal to pay her price, or she can elect to sever her relationship from a person she feels is irresponsible and irredeemably in her debt. Either way, Paul has escaped from the debt through his declaration of emotional bankruptcy.

DEBT FLIGHT: UNILATERAL WITHDRAWAL BY THE DEBTOR

Some emotional debts become so burdensome that entrapped debtors feel they must remove themselves from the reach of their creditors or be crushed under the weight of unending repayment. In such cases, the debtor may decide that physical separation from the creditor becomes the only means for preserving sanity and survival. Either the overbearing demands of a relentless creditor can drive the debtor to take flight, or the very nature of the required compensation may be so difficult or abhorrent that the debtor cannot even contemplate remaining in the midst of what for him is an intolerable situation. When such a point is reached, rightly or wrongly, fleeing may seem the only rational choice for the besieged debtor.

There are even times when unilateral flight from emotional debt is not simply an option, but becomes a valid necessity for protecting against total emotional breakdown. The prime example is when a debtor is shackled by an unyielding creditor who is intent on extracting interminable payment as a means of punishment or control. In such situations, the creditor has set a repayment schedule that is tantamount to a "life sentence without parole." The following case of Henry and Lily vividly portrays how a frustrated debtor decides to take flight.

Henry accepted a job promotion six years ago which forced his family to move out to the West coast and leave their roots in the East. It was a hard transition for their three children, but even harder for his wife Lily who had lived her entire life in Connecticut. After the move, she went into a serious depression and became increasingly hostile towards him for having "ruined her entire life." She felt cutoff from her mother and father, her closest friends and all of her lifelong emotional ties. Lily was lonely and drifting without any sense of purpose, and she blamed her alienation on her husband's selfishness.

Henry tried to empathize and compensate her for her loss, but it became clear that nothing he could do would stop Lily from blaming him. Any of his efforts to appease her were rebuffed and she persisted in her hostile attitude of resentment. Henry came to realize that Lily was never going to relinquish her need to punish him.

Henry expressed his resignation. "I've reached the point where I really believe that it is a hopeless situation. Our youngest son is off to college in the fall, and as soon as he is settled I have decided to file for a divorce. Lily will go ballistic when I tell her, but I'm not willing to go on in a relationship where my wife's only apparent goal is to make me suffer for something I had to do six years ago. I know she will continue to try to make life miserable for me through the divorce, but I've already spoken with an attorney and know pretty much what I am facing. It's hard to leave a twenty-four-year marriage, but I'm not willing to put up with her anger any longer. I feel like leaving is my only real option."

Henry's assessment of his predicament was based in reality. An interview with Lily confirmed her entrenchment—her agenda was to extract the maximum punishment possible. There was absolutely no willingness on her part either to pursue a reasonable settlement or to consider forgiveness as an avenue for resolution. Henry's decision to flee the unpayable debt may well be his healthiest alternative.

Flight from a relentless creditor is sometimes the only reasonable alternative for a hopelessly entrapped debtor.

There are, of course, many situations when a debtor will flee a situation which is not truly irreconcilable. Such a debtor may choose to flee out of fear, stubbornness or pure selfishness rather than as a measure of self-preservation. Such unilateral withdrawal may not be noble or commendable, but it is nevertheless an option for the debtor who feels he cannot face the burden of repayment. But debt flight, regardless of the reason, permanently severs the existing relationship. From the outside, fleeing a debt may look like an inexpensive and easy way out, but the relationship is always lost and that cost is inescapable.

UNRESOLVABLE DEBTS

There are certain types of relational debts which by their very nature defy resolution. These debts are so extreme that no form of repayment will ever be sufficient. Unresolvable debts can evolve in two different ways: 1) positive acts of such magnitude that they can never be compensated, and 2) violations so heinous that they can never be atoned for or forgiven.

Positive Acts Which Cannot Be Paid Back:

- John throws himself on a live grenade and saves Peter's life.

- Tanya donates a kidney to her younger sister.

- Edgar runs into a neighbor's burning home to rescue her baby daughter.

- Gayle learns that her parents adopted her even though she is severely disabled.

- Mark escapes his lethal heroine addiction after his best friend commandeers him into a rehabilitation clinic.

Anyone who has ever been on the receiving end of such dramatic, selfless outpourings of care can never find adequate means for expressing and resolving the depth of his gratitude. Such debtors feel as though nothing they can do will ever sufficiently repay their creditors. The actual creditors may or may not perceive any existing debt, but the heroic dimension of their actions leaves the recipients eternally thankful. Individuals frequently feel this kind of debt towards their parents, siblings, other relatives, certain teachers or mentors, special friends or lovers. Often, the best repayment possible is a genuine "thank you" which may be more than sufficient to the creditor, although it will usually feel terribly inadequate to the debtor. These are debts which the debtor can never fully relinquish. They will be borne throughout life either as nagging weights of guilt or as familiar reminders that certain acts of human compassion can always transcend our normal need for relational equity.

Unredeemable and Unforgivable Violations:

- Joan's daughter is killed by a drunk driver.

- Paul's business partner cheats Paul out of his entire fortune.

- Calvin lost his hearing as a child from beatings he suffered.

- Sharon was sexually molested by her uncle.

- Jerry's father abandoned the family when Jerry was two.

Drastic debts which emanate from such horrific traumas create impenetrable senses of emotional debt. Creditors who are victimized by such experiences carry ledgers of debt which are beyond restitution or forgiveness. The agony and scars from such extreme betrayals and violations can never be set right.

Of course, no specific act is, in and of itself, inherently unforgivable; but forgiveness is always dependent on the capacity of the creditor, and all creditors on this earthly plane have their limits. Creditors in these excruciating situations may never be able to relinquish their resentment whether or not the offending debtor feels remorse or seeks ways to repay. No amount of repayment will ever fill the gaping hole of loss which the injured creditor must bear. They may have to carry the debt to their grave.

DEBT CANCELLATION

Because relational debts can be present solely due to perception, the process of debt identification can lead to the discovery that it is only the debtor who perceives the debt. The person to whom the debtor feels something is owed (the perceived creditor) may simply not share the notion that any compensation is warranted. Upon being apprised of the debt, the surprised creditor can assure the debtor that there is no need for any compensation. In such a case, the debtor is released from the burden of debt through the process of simple debt cancellation.

With debt cancellation, forgiveness is not at issue because, in the mind of the creditor, there is nothing to forgive. The debt is dissolved through the understanding that, to the creditor, there was no meaningful debt in the first place. Scott and Kimberly's situation provides a good example of debt cancellation.

> After weeks of stewing, Kimberly came to her husband Scott and revealed that she had been feeling guilty over an incident she had never told him about. Scott had no idea what she was referring to or why she was so upset, so he sat down with her and let her pour out her story.
>
> "A year and a half ago," Kimberly said, "when you were out of town on a business trip, I got a call from my old boyfriend, Mark. He said he was going to be here in the area and wanted to know if we could

get together for dinner. I agreed to meet him in the city. It all seemed innocent enough at first.

"Well, I realized as the time drew near how excited I was to see him. I put on my favorite black dress and spent the afternoon getting ready . . . I felt like a high school girl all over again.

"The moment Mark and I saw each other, we could both tell that the energy was still there. We had a nice dinner, wine, after-dinner drinks—and then he invited me back to his hotel room. I knew it was wrong, but I drove to his hotel and fantasized about what making love with him would be like again.

"When I arrived, he met me in the lobby . . . but I just couldn't go through with it. I gave him a hug and ran back out to my car in tears. I couldn't believe I was that close to giving in. It scared me so much.

"I never told you about any of this before. I guess I felt too ashamed and was afraid of how upset you would be. But the guilt has been killing me. I can't keep living with the lie. I'm so sorry. I'm sorry for what I did and I'm sorry for not telling you about it when it all happened. Can you forgive me?"

Scott took Kimberly's hand, squeezed it gently and said to her, "Kimberly, apart from not telling me about this earlier, I don't see that you've done anything wrong. I don't expect you to never spend time with other men or that you will never be attracted to anyone else. You and Mark had a long, intense relationship. I've gotten over that a long time ago and I trust your commitment to me. Turning away from him and leaving the hotel was a real show of your devotion. Your decision to not have an affair with Mark is what's important. You didn't do anything wrong, so far as I'm concerned, there's nothing to forgive."

After having Kimberly explain her sense of debt, Scott was surprised at her level of emotional distress. His view of the situation does not attribute blame to his wife in the same way that she attributes blame to herself. Still, Kimberly's guilt defines the debt and Scott's willingness to discharge the debt freely allows her to experience full release. Whereas debt forgiveness always requires a blameworthy offender, debt cancellation can serve to dismiss perceived violations and resolve the experience of guilt. Blame is not a determining factor because the creditor perceives either that there was nothing to blame in the first place, or that the infraction was so slight as to be inconsequential. Scott's cancellation of Kimberly's debt emanates from his perspective and insight rather than his need to resolve any perceived injustice. In debt cancellation, it is the debtor who benefits most, since Scott, as creditor, has no resentment which requires resolution.

CONCLUSION

Though debt resolution is the objective for partners trying to reach a mutual satisfaction, emotional debts cannot always be paid off or forgiven. When the debt is too great or the dictated terms of repayment too high, emotional debtors may need to escape through "emotional bankruptcy"—the declaration of an unwillingness or inability to pay. We have also seen how "debt flight"—running away from the situation entirely—is another option for over-burdened partners facing unpayable debts.

Emotional debts can also be discharged unilaterally by a creditor who declares the debtor's perception of debt invalid or unnecessary. This type of "debt cancellation" frees the emotional debtor from any obligation or duty to repay.

Finally, we have examined certain emotional debts which by their very nature are unresolvable. Certain acts of heroism or extreme generosity may create debts that simply can never be paid back. In the same vein, heinous acts of betrayal or abuse can create victimized creditors who will never be satisfied by any amount of restitution and who may never be able to offer forgiveness for the harm suffered.

Therefore, though there are some debts which cannot be resolved, the spectrum of attainable debt resolution ranges from debt settlement to debt forgiveness to debt escapes. When emotional debts are finally and fully resolved, partners can be freed to pursue growth and intimacy without the shackles of debt holding them back.

Chapter 10

BEING EVEN
The Ultimate Balance in Relationships

"Neither a borrower nor a lender be."
- Shakespeare

Once freed of emotional debt, a whole new concept of intimate relationships emerges—Being Even. With the framework of debt resolution in mind, we can now explore in depth the richness and healthy balance possible in relationships that possess no hidden debts—relationships that operate with spontaneity, free exchange, unforced caring and true intimacy . . . relationships which are truly EVEN.

Through the integration of two opposite ways of viewing relationships, a surprising, new framework emerges which not only promotes understanding but also stimulates growth and vitality. This synthesis evolves from a consideration of two polar models of how people approach relational interactions— from relational scorekeeping on one end of the spectrum to idealistic, unconditional love on the other end. In order to unveil our new blueprint for intimacy, we must first look at each of the polar extremes which set the parameters for how partners interact.

TWO OPPOSITE MODELS OF RELATIONSHIPS: SCOREKEEPING VS. UNCONDITIONAL LOVE

At one end of the relationship spectrum is scorekeeping in which each partner constantly keeps a score sheet of who owes whom. It is a strictly mechanical scorekeeping approach to relationships which centers on the idea of equalizing debits and credits at all times—"I'll only do for you if you do for me." Every act, no matter how small, requires a response of equal weight. When I vacuum the carpets, it must be reciprocated by you doing the dishes or some chore of equal value. If I purchase a new car for the family, then you must pay for the home remodeling project—chore for chore, dollar for dollar, tit-for-tat.

Those caught up in a scorekeeping relationship soon voice protests such as:

- *"I can't stand being in a relationship where you're always keeping a tally."*

- *"I don't want to bicker over every little thing."*

- *"Whatever happened to the simple idea of giving without always having to get something in return?"*

- *"This feels more like a business arrangement than a love relationship."*

Such objections are valid when assessing a scorekeeping approach to a relationship. Trying to maintain equality in all ways at all times in intimate relationships is a distasteful and eventually unsatisfying mode of intimate connection. Such false equality can only produce negative energy. Individuals entrapped in such a balance sheet relationship never seem to get beyond the hair-trigger tension, suspicion and uneasiness that are the unavoidable side effects of such an arrangement. The pitfalls of a scorekeeping relationship are painfully evident. Who would opt for the prickly feelings of edginess, the pervasive spirit of competitiveness, the constant sense of unfairness, the stifling attitude of always having to:

- *Watch out for your own interests.*

- *Have your every action scrutinized under a microscope.*

- Keep a watchful eye on your partner.

- Weigh and balance every tiny favor or minute transgression.

In an effort to uphold precise equality, compassion and the higher potential of the human spirit are brutally sacrificed.

The opposite extreme to such a balance sheet approach is the widely embraced and emotionally seductive notion of unconditional love. The model of unconditional love presumes that both participants give selflessly without any expectation of receiving something in return. Concepts of balance, fairness and equality are superseded by the overarching virtue of unselfish love—giving to others without the need for acknowledgment, gratitude or repayment. While this glowing ideal of unreciprocated giving may seem a noble pursuit, the very nature of human relationships makes some degree of give-and-take inevitable. It is natural to give to others from areas of personal strength; but wholeness can only be achieved when we allow ourselves to openly receive what others have to offer us as well.

When carried out to its ultimate conclusions, unconditional love exposes itself as unrealistic and, in actuality, not at all the virtuous ideal it promised to be. Real love must be rooted in the full acceptance of our human nature and a vibrant recognition of our individual differences. The undeniable rhythms of all human beings involve some periods of natural outreach and giving alternating with times of withdrawal and need. Unconditional love, once demystified from its glorified sanctity, represents a denial of our basic human impulses and a defacement of our true nature.

The expression of our distinctive personalities is rooted in the recognition of our unique needs and individual aspirations. When unconditional love becomes an obliteration of another person's personality or a denial of our human nature, then a logical contradiction arises—can we authentically love another while sacrificing the integrity of our own personhood? It is one thing to try to accept someone for who they are, with all of their differences and flaws, and another to negate the reality of our own needs, values and emotions.

**Identity suicide is never the path
to genuine human connection.**

The New Testament imperative "to love others as ourselves" is not just a commandment—it also is a natural law, a statement of fact about our ability to love. Only by recognizing and embracing our uniqueness and value can we genuinely share in the lives of others. We must love ourselves before it is possible to love others. Sacrificing our humanity and personality cannot be the means to attain true love; conflict avoidance can never be a vehicle for genuine bonding; and unconditional love can never supplant the richness and vitality of human diversity as the basis for authentic intimacy in relationships.

THE CONTINUUM OF RELATIONAL POSSIBILITIES

Obviously there are severe limitations to both the extreme model of relational scorekeeping and the idealistic paradigm of unconditional love. If we look at a continuum representing the spectrum of relational possibilities, pure relational scorekeeping and total unconditional love constitute the polar extremes:

```
RELATIONAL                              UNCONDITIONAL
SCOREKEEPING                                LOVE
+----------------------+----------------------+
                    midpoint
```

All relationships fall somewhere along this line based on the dynamic of interaction. Neither extreme—relational scorekeeping nor unconditional love—represents a desirable or practical model of relationship. However, there are positive aspects which can be extracted from each mode of relating—the practical necessity of give-and-take found in the scorekeeping approach and the acceptance and willing compromise embedded in the notion of unconditional love. What is needed is a synthesis of the valuable qualities inherent in both extremes. The integration of the pragmatic with the ideal is embodied in a new relational model which I term, *Being Even*.

WHAT IT MEANS TO BE EVEN

Being Even in a relationship means being debt free. Evenness implies the absence of resentments harbored by unpaid creditors and the freedom from guilt hanging over the head of weary debtors.

Being Even has absolutely nothing to do with the notion of *getting even*, with the implication of revenge or reprisal. Rather than focusing on punitive retribution, Being Even is an affirming concept which honors the highest capacities of our human nature. The narrow, mean-spirited attempt to get even is so antithetical to the uplifting experience of Being Even that the pursuit of either one automatically nullifies any possibility of achieving the other.

Just as being a debtor or a creditor is a matter of perception, Being Even is defined by the perception that nothing is owed by either partner. Being Even requires no proof or reason—it transcends logic, external evidence and all conceptual systems of parity. The perception of Evenness emerges as an encompassing feeling of trust, enthusiasm and peace of mind. Once all relational debts have been resolved, there is no longer any remnant of guilt, resentment or the uncomfortable anticipatory anxiety of waiting for the emotional ax to fall.

When each partner in a relationship is Even, there is a mutual sense of balance and fairness that allows for the broadest range of unencumbered giving. A natural flow of give-and-take exchange can occur without the need for exact accounting or measure-for-measure scrutiny. It is a state in which each partner can operate with a maximum sense of freedom, spontaneity and security.

**When individuals feel Even, kindness and appreciation
radiate without effort, small offenses go unnoticed,
human frailties are tolerated with grace and
compassion and intimate connections occur naturally.**

Evenness is radically different than a scorekeeping approach to relationships. In strict balance sheet partnerships, every action carries a significant weight. Neither partner can either give or receive without the delicate balance being upset. Fleeting nanoseconds of equality occur as momentary *points* of balance, with every interaction ripe with potential for disturbing the fragile symmetry and sending the relationship teetering.

EXACT SCOREKEEPING

Partner 1 ——————————————◆——————————————— Partner 2

BALANCE POINT

Being Even is radically different from scorekeeping in its depth and reach. Scorekeeping is always a self-defeating process which requires the recalibration of the relationship to a point of balance through a continuous sequence of tit-for-tat exchanges. It is a tedious, frustrating progression in which every action and reaction must be carefully calculated, weighed and accounted for. Spontaneity and free giving are sacrificed at the altar of demonstrable equality.

Being Even, on the other hand, is not simply a function of totaling up the pluses and minuses on an emotional ledger board and calculating a net sum which provides an objective impression of equality. In fact, such a petty, mechanical approach is antithetical to allowing the natural balance of true Evenness to expand over time. When people are freed from artificially attempting to keep things equal at every moment, then the spontaneous flow of giving and receiving can take place with both parties maintaining an internal sense of everything being fair.

In a relationship suffused with a mutual feeling of Evenness, balance is preserved by a wide *base* of debtlessness rather than a hairline *point*:

BEING EVEN

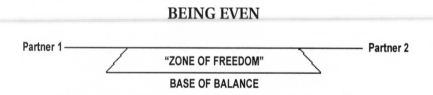

The experience of Evenness is determined by a broad *Zone of Freedom* in which partners are liberated to spontaneously give and receive without the need for tallying or reciprocity. When Evenness flourishes and the Zone of Freedom is wide, giving does not create a demand for recompense and receiving does not result in a need to repay. Within the Zone of Freedom, debts do not arise. Relational balance is maintained in a shared gratitude for being together with a mutual sense of trust, and not by a conscious weighing of one favor for another.

The Zone of Freedom serves two important functions: 1) it defines the parameters within which debt-free exchange can occur, and 2) it forms a sturdy base so that actions outside the Zone of Freedom are less likely to destabilize the relationship.

> When partners are able to achieve a wide Zone of
> Freedom, comfort and trust will flourish and actions
> outside the Zone can be more effectively managed.

Within the Zone of Freedom, generous giving and gracious receiving become an achievable reality. Partners who feel debt-free—who perceive that they are neither owed anything nor carry significant debt—are able to engage in unselfish exchanges which embrace the spirit of authentic human love. However, the pragmatic reality of Evenness also incorporates the undeniable fact that there are always limits to unreciprocated giving. These limits are defined by the boundaries which designate the Zone of Freedom. Outside of these parameters, give-or-take exchanges are, in fact, subject to conditions which need to be acknowledged and negotiated.

> Evenness combines the spirit of selfless love with the
> necessity of fulfilling our own needs and desires.

Most of us have experienced levels of Evenness in certain kinds of relationships. For instance, some of us have maintained a best friend from childhood where the bond of friendship has endured through adult life. Because of the years of history and shared experiences together, such life-long friendships rest on sturdy foundations of trust slowly cured by time. Petty squabbles, minor slights and even the occasional heated disagreement are easily accommodated within the greater perception that everything will even out in the long run. The passage of time in itself tends to solidify and broaden the Zone of Freedom in relationships which begin and develop in positive ways.

Another recognizable experience of Evenness can be observed in siblings who have grown up with physically abusive parents. The shared ordeal of having to endure and survive ongoing stress and trauma can forge powerful allegiances which create unshakable trust and support. To children who suffer together through such intense travail, the strength of their connection cannot be frayed by such meager considerations as who gets to play the video game or whose turn it is to feed the dog. In such relationships, it is the intensity of the shared circumstances which serves to expand the Zone of Freedom and foster an ongoing

sense of fairness and balance. Other situations can be spring-
boards to Evenness through shared experience, such as soldiers in
combat, survivors of a natural disaster, medical students enduring their residency or even workmates successfully accomplishing
major projects.

Another important way that Evenness can be established
and the Zone of Freedom widened is through the successful resolution of existing debts. Whether resolution is achieved through
agreement and payment or by means of forgiveness, debt settlements do not occur in isolation. Instead, there is a cumulative
effect in which each successive debt settlement builds faith and
trust. This paves the way for more expedient resolutions in the
future. The experience of Being Even builds upon itself—as confidence in the relationship and a sense of security and fairness flourish, partners can experience an ever-growing Zone of Freedom.

However Evenness takes root and blossoms—whether
through time, shared experience or the successful resolution of
existing debts—it is always a fluid and dynamic process that continually maintains a shifting sense of balance between people.
Being Even is not a static state, something to be achieved and
then left unattended. The goal is not to reach some set point of
equilibrium or some changeless plateau of relational nirvana.
Instead, Evenness requires mindful vigilance so that individuals
can continue to live out richly textured relationships at their highest potential by constantly expanding the region of trust, freedom
and intimacy.

The Evidence of Evenness

In the same manner that relational debts are evidenced by emotional symptoms such as guilt, resentment, frustration and anger,
relationships which are Even are also characterized by visible
signs and feelings. When partners perceive that they are debt-free
and Even, they feel safe and secure, appreciative and appreciated,
more spontaneous, less guarded and more vigorously engaged in
the process of living. Because there is an absence of niggling
squabbles, competitive maneuvering and deadening blame, individuals can freely risk their own vulnerability, thereby pushing
the outer limits of their self-expression. When couples feel Even,
their relationship resonates with expanding intimacy since there

is a firm basis for uninhibited self-disclosure and a congruent expression of authentic emotion.

The vitalizing spirit which embodies Evenness typifies the best part of close relationships—the feeling that virtually all things are possible and the excitement of gazing out upon a limitless horizon together.

PRESERVING EVENNESS OUTSIDE THE ZONE OF FREEDOM THROUGH DEBT MANAGEMENT

Within their personal Zone of Freedom, partners spontaneously operate in natural and free manners—giving and receiving unself-consciously without any strings attached or hooks dangling. However, when issues extend beyond the boundaries of the existing Zone of Freedom, partners are thrust into the precarious outer regions where debts arise and threaten to destabilize the relationship.

OUTSIDE THE ZONE OF FREEDOM

Partner 1 ——————————————————————— Partner 2
REGION OF POTENTIAL DEBT   **ZONE OF FREEDOM**   *REGION OF POTENTIAL DEBT*

When couples venture into the Region of Potential Debt, there is a strong risk that new indebtedness can arise and fracture the sense of Evenness, thus forcing the relationship out of balance. Outside of the security of unencumbered exchange afforded by the Zone of Freedom, any giving and receiving has the potential for incurring a burden of debt. Emotions of uneasiness, restlessness, doubt and fear are all initial indicators that the realm of probable debt has been penetrated. If couples manage to retreat from the danger zones of debt and Evenness is restored, the pre-existing Zone of Freedom may have dramatically shrunk from the fallout.

The irony is that only through a willingness and courage to venture into the Regions of Potential Debt can a relationship mature and deepen. Couples often try to avoid any gray areas and potential pitfalls by tightly restraining the relationship within the confines of the *existing* Zone of Freedom. Relationships are stunted and immobilized by rationalizations such as:

- "We're getting along fine—why risk rocking the boat."

- "Don't do anything that might damage what we've already built."

- "I better wait for the right time to bring it up"

- "If I tell her the truth she's bound to be angry."

- "Better safe than sorry."

The paradox of attempting to preserve a static Zone of Freedom is that such efforts inevitably lead to the atrophy of the Zone. Relational maturity is a product of acknowledging the risks of future debt while still pushing against the boundaries of complacency and routine interaction. Like a living organism, the Zone of Freedom must grow and expand or it is destined to shrivel.

The alternative to a shallow security based on "playing it safe" is the courage to risk growth. However, such risk should not be undertaken with wild abandon, blindness or naïve disregard.

It is always wise to strategically reduce the riskiness of relational risk.

While partners must be adventurous in order to promote thriving growth, maturity is also reflected through mindful attentiveness and anticipation of situations ripe with the potential for debt. The challenge of maintaining Evenness on the outskirts of the Zone of Freedom demands assiduous debt management. Two methods for tempering risk while living on the relational edge are Debt Prevention and Up-front Debt Agreements.

DEBT PREVENTION

Sometimes it is much easier to avoid debts in the first place rather than being forced to resolve them once they have formed. The prevention of debts requires alertness and anticipation of situations that have high potential for creating emotional debt. Individuals must be brutally honest with themselves and their partners when they sense they are entering areas where they are predisposed to becoming creditors or debtors. Foreseeing a potential stumbling block of debt can lead to a forthright discussion which addresses the issue before the debt is incurred. The success of Tony and Susan provides an example of debt prevention.

Tony was scheduled to go on a business trip to the East Coast. He decided he wanted to extend the trip for three days so he could go hiking with his brother in Maine. He considered telling his wife Susan that his business trip would be three days longer than it actually was. He rationalized that it would be easier to just sidestep the issue and avoid conflict.

After reflecting on his plan, Tony realized that he would end up feeling guilty (*risk becoming a DEBTOR*) if he lied to his wife. He considered taking Susan along, but in his heart he knew that he really wanted to spend the time alone with his brother. To take Susan with him, even though he actually preferred to go alone, would create the possibility of feeling resentful (*becoming a CREDITOR*).

Tony was prepared to make a bargain with Susan in order to fulfill his desire to spend time alone with his brother. He was willing to pay for her to visit her sister while he was away in Maine. He approached his wife with a clear, direct communication about his desire to spend time alone with his brother. He offered the compensatory trip to Susan and was surprised by her reaction.

"That sounds fine," Susan told Tony. "I'm glad you'll get to spend some private time with your brother. But, to tell you the truth I don't really want to go anywhere—I would cherish a few days to myself here at home."

Tony's straightforward communication set the stage for getting what he wanted while incurring no debt in the process. Clearly he took a risk in addressing the issue directly—Susan may have had other plans for them or may have been angry over his desire to be away from her—but neither proved to be the case. He was even prepared to negotiate an exchange in order to get the time with his brother, but, as things turned out, no exchange was required. Susan demanded nothing in return. No debt was ever created and no payment was necessary. The fact that potential debt can be anticipated and avoided allows Evenness to thrive.

**Clear, open and direct communication is
the most effective tool for debt prevention.**

Up-Front Debt Agreements

Although Being Even implies being debt-free, it is possible for Evenness to be maintained in the presence of a conscious creation of a new debt. To preserve Evenness, both partners must acknowledge that new debt is being taken on and must mutually negotiate the terms of repayment before the debt is solidified. A conscious agreement by both the creditor and the debtor creates a temporary debt with a pre-determined method and time frame for settlement. In such a case, the nature of the debt and the precise terms of payment need to be explicitly set forth and agreed to ahead of time. The fact that both parties *willingly* enter into such a debt agreement allows the relationship to retain the spirit of Evenness in spite of the pre-arranged debt. Karen and Al's use of an up-front debt agreement demonstrates how balance can be maintained.

Karen wanted Al to attend her twenty-year high school reunion. Al had no desire whatsoever to be in a large social situation with a mass of people he didn't know. Furthermore, he was not interested in meeting any of Karen's old boyfriends—two of whom had been long-term, sexual partners. Karen pleaded with Al to go with her. She told him that she would feel awkward going alone and that she wanted to share the most important part of her life with her friends from the past. As a means of getting what she wanted, Karen eventually agreed to take on an acceptable debt.

Their up-front debt agreement took a very specific form. Al agreed to accompany Karen to her reunion. They arranged transportation so Al could leave early following the big dinner. Furthermore, Karen agreed that next summer she and Al would spend their vacation fishing in Alaska where Al had always dreamed of going. Karen is not wild about fishing or the thought of a week in the wilderness, but was willing to venture there next year in exchange for having Al attend part of her reunion. Both partners feel satisfied with their ends of the bargain.

After attending the reunion Al will become a predetermined creditor. Karen (the willing debtor) owes him the trip to Alaska (debt payment) in one year (schedule of repayment). The fact that the debt has been mutually agreed upon up-front allows the relationship to remain Even. And simply maintaining Evenness is not the only benefit. By successfully working out an agreement about the debt in advance, Karen and Al set themselves up for maximum enjoyment of both experiences (the reunion and the Alaska trip), because guilt and resentment have not been allowed to poison the atmosphere.

Up-front debt negotiation provides an open channel for give-and-take so that relational Evenness can be preserved.

The fact that Al and Karen have been able to successfully complete a process of debt negotiation also may have a profound impact on the dimensions of their relationship's Zone of Freedom. The backdrop of trust that emerges from their up-front agreement creates an environment of mutual appreciation in which their Zone of Freedom can expand.

CONCLUSION

Being Even is the most powerful force in human relationships. It is an unfolding, ever-changing process of relational development, trust and respect. Because Evenness shatters the manacles—obligation, dependency and fear—of debt-ridden relationships, individuals who perceive that they are even and debt-free are able to experience the broadest range of unencumbered giving and receiving.

Evenness is gauged by feelings of confidence, liberation,

comfort and openness. When partners feel even, kindness and appreciation flow, small offenses go unnoticed, human frailties are tolerated with grace and compassion and intimate connections occur naturally.

The full value of the vocabulary and conceptual framework of relational debt is that it ultimately leads to a vivid understanding of that most precious feeling of freedom and fulfillment—the feeling of Being Even. The language of emotional debt is not an end in itself, but a passage to the meaningful experience of Being Even.

Chapter 11

LIBERATION COMES TO LIFE
Achieving and Maintaining Evenness:
A Couple Study

"Life is just one damn thing after another."
- Elbert Hubbard

"It is not true that life is one damn thing after another—
it is one damn thing over and over."
- Edna St. Vincent Millay

For six years, nearly the entire length of their marriage, Mark and Denise sensed something was wrong. On the surface their relationship functioned smoothly—both had stable jobs, they had recently purchased their first home, they teamed up effectively at executing the daily activities of household management (meals, finances, shopping, chores) and enjoyed an extended network of family and friends. In many ways the relationship appeared not only solid, but almost ideal. No one would have suspected that this was a marriage in need of help.

In spite of their superficial harmony, there was a submerged current of discontent that ran through their daily life together. It was as if each partner suffered from an unspoken, low-grade depression about his or her relationship, a dull despondency which drained their interactions of life, energy and all intimacy. Neither partner spoke openly about his or her disappointment to one another or even to close friends. Mark and Denise had no immediate recognition of the issues or driving force behind the relationship's wearying distress because neither partner's full discontent had risen to a level of conscious awareness. Their tension hovered like an invisible fog, mute and colorless, but always distorting their communication and sapping the marriage of all passion.

Denise's and Mark's dissatisfaction rarely manifested in public. They had an unspoken agreement about preserving their image as a loving couple—both of them unconsciously colluding to uphold the facade of bliss. There were numerous occasions when resentments would threaten to erupt, but the couple would quickly pull things together to go through the motions of a social situation with their image intact. Conflicts would be postponed or swept under the rug as often as possible for the sake of maintaining their own visions of a peaceful and stable relationship.

The long-existing pattern involved prolonged periods of distant edginess, punctuated by outbursts of anger and blame. Their responses to the underlying distress took different forms—Mark tended to withdraw and sulk while Denise was more direct and outspoken about her upset. Whenever tensions boiled over, the pattern was for Mark to retreat while Denise made futile and aggressive attempts to draw him out. Eventually, Denise would give up and would withdraw to silently stew in her own anger and disgust.

Sometimes the couple would attempt to pinpoint the triggering issues of dispute, but there was rarely any mutual feeling of agreement about the precipitating events let alone any sense of resolution. The underlying problems were never reached. After a flare-up, it took about twenty-four hours for Mark and Denise to approach one another and make-up. Reconciliation involved apologies, a re-affirmation of their care and commitment, and a sexual reunion. The relationship would return to its functional plane, but the hidden toxins eating away at the relationship were never exposed or neutralized. Their relational virus would retreat and become dormant for a while, but it was never too long before the marriage would suffer from yet another outbreak of surface symptoms.

Finally, the impetus for change came about in an unexpected and tragic way. Denise's father, who was only fifty-six, had a sudden heart attack and died. The shocking loss had reverberating consequences for Denise and her entire family, but as crises often do, the event jolted Denise out of her complacency and denial and became the springboard for real transformation.

Her father's death brought a cascade of feelings crashing down upon her. Her normal coping mechanisms failed from overload and Denise became distraught, confused and disoriented. Her emotions had never been so out of control and she had never felt so vulnerable. With her defensive structure blown away, Denise knew she needed help. On the recommendation of her best friend, she sought the help of a professional therapist.

Denise's counseling initially was focused on the loss of her father. As her emotional bearings were slowly restored and as she worked through her grief, other feelings emerged not only about her relationship with her father but also concerning tensions with her husband. What emerged was a realization that Denise held a deep resentment against Mark that tied into her history with her father.

When Denise was fourteen, her father had taken a job that forced the family to move from Memphis to central Oregon. The uprooting and relocation had been traumatic for Denise. She left behind lifetime friends, had to start at a new high school, was forced to break off a relationship with a boyfriend and had to adjust to a new rural culture that she didn't like. She protested the move, but her parents saw no alternatives at the time. Denise eventually came to accept the change as best she could. However, as soon as she graduated from high school, she headed back to Tennessee to attend college and had intentions of settling there for good.

Mark and Denise had met at Memphis State and were married the year after they graduated. Denise took an advertising job, but Mark had strong aspirations to go to business school. He applied in the Memphis area, but really wanted to go to Wharton in Pennsylvania. Denise had made it clear that she did not want to leave Tennessee, but when Mark got his acceptance to Wharton he leveraged Denise into moving with assurances of a return to Memphis in the future. After three years in Pennsylvania, however, Mark's only solid job offer came from northern California. Thus the couple relocated and have remained in California ever since.

Denise believed that she had fully accepted the moves to Pennsylvania and San Francisco as necessary sacrifices, but in the course of treatment she began to realize that she harbored ongoing resentment towards Mark due to these imposed uprootings. She also realized that her anger at Mark was exacerbated by the unresolved bitterness she carried from the forced move to Oregon with her first family when she was a teenager.

What ignited Denise's insight was learning about the language of emotional debt. This injected a new perspective. She began to utilize it to interpret her past experiences and ongoing feelings. Now she understood the linkage between her vague feelings of resentment and what previously seemed to be unrelated life events.

Denise observed, "To be honest, I've never thought about Mark owing me anything, but the fact is I've been holding this tremendous resentment. He did promise we would go back to Memphis, but then, when his only job option was here in San Francisco, he acted like we didn't have any choice. I bought into that, I guess. I remember being angry, but more at the circumstances than at Mark. I hate to admit it, but I guess I do feel he owes me something for the sacrifice I made leaving my roots in Tennessee."

"Do you think Mark believes he owes you a debt?" I asked.

Denise shook her head. "I'm not sure. I doubt he does. I think he feels that we were simply victims of circumstances that were beyond his control."

I looked searchingly at her. "But didn't he promise that eventually you would return to Memphis?"

"Yes, but the subject was just dropped. We never discussed Memphis since moving here. It is like someone's child died and nobody dares to talk about it."

"Do you still have hopes of returning to Tennessee someday?"

"No," Denise looked downcast. "I don't think I could face the disappointment again. It has been too painful letting go of my dream. I just try to block it out and accept living here in San Francisco. But the truth is, I really have been angry with Mark about this for a long time. I've just never seen it clearly before now. I think it's all been complicated by how upset I was when my family moved to Oregon when I was a kid. It's hard to sort out my feelings from both situations."

Denise came to the realization that she perceived there to be a tremendous debt owed to her over the moves she was forced to make as well as over Mark's unfulfilled promises of returning to

Memphis. She was able to see that her status as a creditor was compounded and intensified by the unresolved debt with her own father which she also carried from her childhood dislocation. Denise could see that she viewed both Mark and her father as debtors. She doubted that either one of them ever thought of themselves as owing her anything based on decisions they felt obligated to make in their own lives. With her father now dead, Denise had to come to terms with the fact that his debt to her would never be acknowledged or repaid. She would have to seek resolution on her own for the resentment she held about her family's move to Oregon.

With Mark, however, Denise had the opportunity to deal with her perceived debt directly. On her initial attempt to talk with Mark, he reverted to his typical pattern of withdrawal as a means of conflict avoidance. Denise pursued him, but he remained defensive and would not acknowledge the debt she felt he owed to her.

"That was years ago, Denise," Mark said obstinately, poised for a fight. "We did what we had to do and ended up living here. You were part of all those decisions. I don't think it's fair for you to feel the way you do. How can you possibly think I would owe you anything now?"

After a good deal of frustration, Denise was able to get Mark to come to one of her therapy sessions. Finally, Mark was able to step outside himself to understand why Denise felt the way she did.

"I thought the Memphis issue was put to rest long ago, but I can see that Denise still feels resentment over how things ended up. But where does that leave us? Do you expect me to quit my job so that we can move back to Memphis now?" Mark asked soberly.

Denise tried to make her own feelings known once and for all, "No, that's not what I expect at all."

"Then what?"

I wanted both partners to feel comfortable expressing themselves. "Mark, you sound like you're willing to try to settle things."

Mark bit his lip pensively. "Of course. I think this whole thing has been hanging over our marriage far too long. I've never admitted it before, but if I was completely honest, I'd have to confess that I've felt a lot of guilt over forcing Denise to leave Tennessee."

"Then why didn't you ever say anything?" Denise asked, her own strong feelings rising to the surface.

"Why didn't you?" Mark countered. "I always thought avoiding the topic made things easier."

Once again I tried to posit the interchange. "So at some point you actually felt that you did owe a debt to Denise."

Mark nodded. "I've never put it in those terms, but I have felt a lot of gnawing guilt over the years. I guess I didn't think there was any real way to repay her for something that I couldn't change."

"Well," I said, smiling at them both, "let's try to figure out how both of you can settle the debt and get on with things in a better way."

Denise and Mark began to have some insight into their whole relational dynamic. The model of debt proved enormously helpful in getting Mark to understand how the buried debt which gripped Denise served to disrupt their marriage. It was also comforting to Mark to see how he had inherited some of the debt from Denise's father. Mark found it more palatable to accept his role as debtor when Denise described how the unresolved debt with her father exaggerated her emotional upset towards Mark. Mark was eager to consider ways of settling his debt with Denise, as long as there were efforts on her part to differentiate his debt from her father's. Mark's acknowledgment of his position as a debtor, in and of itself, greatly aided Denise in her process of releasing her resentment toward him.

The couple was given the assignment of considering possible currencies for debt repayment. Each partner was to come to the next session with his own independent proposal for a settlement. This task was to be the first step toward negotiating an acceptable resolution. Both partners felt a new level of hope and excitement over the prospect of working through the real issues that had haunted their marriage for so long.

However, as is so often the case, initial enthusiasm managed to inadvertently lead Mark astray, setting the stage for an ill-conceived enterprise which became a new crisis. The unexpected blow-up left Mark feeling more confused and frustrated than ever.

Mark explained, "I don't get it. After we talked last week, I admitted I wanted to try to resolve things with Denise, but now she's furious with me again. I just feel like giving up."

"What happened?" I asked gently.

Denise looked upset. "Mark told me on Friday night that he had a surprise for me. He had gone out and booked reservations for us to go to Memphis for my birthday next month. I couldn't believe he could misread the situation so badly."

Mark was none too happy either. "Like I said, I just don't get it. All we talked about last week in here was how much you loved Memphis. I was trying to do exactly what I thought you wanted. I figured it would be a way to start repaying you. I wasn't trying to cause more trouble, believe me."

Denise stroked her chin and finally said in an even tone, "Well going back to Memphis for a 'nice weekend' at this point isn't going to help me feel better. It would only serve to stir up old hurts all over again."

Mark's gesture was unquestionably sincere—it just happened to be sincerely off target. Mark had made the common mistake of trying to pay off his debt with the wrong currency. His well-intentioned effort backfired horribly and left Denise feeling even more misunderstood. Mark's error was jumping too quickly into a problem-solving mode before he had found the right solution (Ready . . . Fire . . . Aim!). He had offered Denise a payment that made sense to him, but not to her. It was clear that Denise would have to participate in determining adequate terms of settlement if the debt was ever to be resolved.

As Denise shared her ideas for acceptable currencies, Mark realized how off-base he had been with his proposed trip to Memphis.

"I realized that just talking about my upset last week helped a lot. Having you understand why I feel the way I do made things a lot better, Mark. But, I did come up with a few ideas of how to settle things once and for all," Denise said quietly.

Mark was more open now. "Let's hear them."

"I've decided on three things. This may sound weird, but what I really want the most is for you to take ballroom dancing lessons with me."

Mark smiled. "That does sound pretty weird. You've never told me you wanted to take dance lessons before."

Denise nodded. "I know, I always thought you would laugh at me and think the idea was stupid. But that's what I would like most. It would give us something new to do together and get us out on a regular basis."

I said quietly, "What do you think, Mark?"

Mark shrugged. "I don't see how it relates to what happened in the past."

"But regardless of that . . .," I posed.

Mark shrugged his shoulders again. "I have no problem with dance lessons. I wouldn't pick ballroom dancing myself, but if that's what she wants, I'm willing to do it . . . So, what were your other two ideas? I'm almost afraid to ask."

"Well," Denise said slowly, "one is that I want some more help around the house. I'd be willing to either have you do more of the chores yourself or else let me bring in a housecleaner two or three times a month. The third request has more to do with our relationship. I need you to stop shutting down emotionally every time I bring up something that bothers me. I need to have you listen to me and respond. I want some assurance you will hang in there with me when I'm upset."

"Well, I'm willing to consider all three of those things," Mark replied. "But, I don't see how any of them will make up for not moving back to Memphis."

"Nothing will ever change what happened, Mark. I realize I need to let go of the past. If you are willing to do these things, I will feel like nothing else is owed."

"Well, I'm happy to give you all three if it will really end this issue once and for all," Mark said.

"It would mean a lot to me," Denise told him.

Mark looked at her. "But can I really trust that the issue won't come up again even though we agree to put it to rest?"

It was time for me to intervene and clear the atmosphere. "Part of Denise's agreement could involve her commitment to not have the issue resurface with you. We could set a ground rule that it would not be fair to throw the past in your face. Any feelings Denise might continue to struggle with would now officially be defined as solely her problem."

Denise sighed heavily. "I think that would be fair. I can't promise never to think about the past or to feel upset about it, but I can promise not to take it out on you any more, directly or indirectly."

Mark looked relieved. "That would take a big load off me."

Mark and Denise worked together to develop a written agreement. The process of carefully crafting a mutually acceptable settlement involved some give and take by the couple, but the debate was actually positive and rewarding rather than dispiriting or stilted. The fact that the debt had been laid bare allowed their discussion to flow openly without a sense of either personal attack or defensive avoidance.

The most difficult part of wording the agreement was defining Denise's third issue about Mark's withdrawal and lack of communication. However, with some help, they finally arrived at a Debt Settlement Agreement:

DEBT SETTLEMENT AGREEMENT

This Debt Settlement Agreement is hereby made between *Mark* (DEBTOR), and *Denise* (CREDITOR). The purpose of the agreement is to fully resolve the debt between the parties which arose over the issue of *Never moving back to Memphis.* As full and final compensation, Debtor agrees to pay and Creditor agrees to accept payment in the form of: *1) Participate with Denise in weekly ballroom dancing lessons for a period of six months. 2) Hire a housecleaner for 6 hours of cleaning every other week. 3) Whenever Denise makes the request that, "she needs to sit down and talk with Mark about something important," he will SIT with her, MAINTAIN EYE CONTACT, LISTEN, REFLECT BACK what he hears, and RESPOND verbally.*

Debtor and Creditor further agree to the following schedule of payment: *1) Start dance lessons within one month. 2) Have housecleaner start within two weeks. 3) Begin communication agreement as of now.*

In the event of delinquency, Debtor agrees to the following consequences: *Return to counseling to discuss reasons for not following through.*

Addendum: *In exchange, Denise, agrees to no longer blame Mark for the moves to Pennsylvania and San Francisco. She promises to never raise these issues directly or indirectly with him, and to independently pursue whatever counseling she may need to help her let go of her resentments from the past.*

Mark Anderson	*4-17-98*
DEBTOR's signature	Date
Denise Anderson	*4-17-98*
CREDITOR's signature	Date

Follow-up sessions with Mark and Denise convincingly demonstrated that their debt settlement had a revitalizing impact on their relationship. Both partners reported a sense of cleansing—as if their relationship had been given a jump-start that recharged their mutual energy and outlook. The experience of defining the pre-existing debt and working together towards a settlement not only served to eradicate Mark and Denise's past problem, but also introduced a new *process* of communication and interaction which the couple began to implement across a wide spectrum of other issues.

Mark summed up his new insights. "I think what has struck me most is realizing just how much of our relationship was played out in my head. I thought we used to communicate pretty well, but I now see how much I filtered out. I realize that I've been afraid to tell Denise lots of things. I'd rule them out before even giving her a chance to react."

Denise smiled approvingly. "We're talking with each other a lot more and telling each other what we really want. I think when I asked Mark to go ballroom dancing with me it opened our eyes. I mean, we have really had fun doing it together. I can't believe I held back asking for that. I guess we've both realized it works a whole lot better telling each other what we want instead of trying to read each other's mind."

Mark interjected, "I'm realizing that if I do say what I want and Denise disagrees, it isn't the end of the world. We've been able to negotiate and compromise on a lot of things that never would have been discussed before. The difference now is that the discussions take place out loud instead of secretly in our own minds."

Mark and Denise began to experience the full meaning of Evenness. They relied on their emotions to be accurate barometers of when the relationship was getting out of balance and when they were at risk of creating new debts. Perhaps the strongest indicator of progress in their relationship was the fact that both partners felt an expanding Zone of Freedom which encouraged the spontaneous blossoming of intimate and loving exchanges:

Denise looked glowing. "I just feel so much better towards Mark in general. There has been a real shift in my level of trust. It's funny, because three months ago I would have said that I trusted Mark, but I really didn't. I couldn't trust him to tell me what he thought or felt; I couldn't trust him to listen or respond to me . . . I think I just pretended we had a good marriage. We were so good at acting it out."

Mark contributed, "The relationship feels much more alive. I'm not avoiding conflicts like I did before. We have more open disagreements than we ever did, but they're positive . . . it's not like we're fighting against each other. We're working as partners, not opponents. Things aren't perfect, but we don't get locked into the old patterns. I don't get afraid of Denise or defensive as much as I used to. I feel a whole lot freer and more appreciative of her." He looked lovingly at Denise. "She really does care for me."

Denise smiled back at her partner. "Both of us are giving more to each other. I know I'm not holding back as much as I used to. I feel like I want to give more to

Mark because I know he is giving more to me. I trust him. I don't have to keep score any more. Things really do feel even."

CONCLUSION

Perfection? No—but Mark and Denise were able to make a dramatic shift and significant steps forward in how they related to and cared for one another. This change was given birth through a new way of looking at their relationship and through a process for resolving past debts and preventing new debts so that a trusting balance of Evenness could emerge naturally. The end product is a new level of hope and satisfaction in their partnership. Mark and Denise can expect setbacks as time goes on, but they are unlikely to relapse into their old patterns of denial, withdrawal and censored communication, because their mutual satisfaction with the relationship they share has grown to new heights.

When the rules of an old game are exposed, it is nearly impossible to go back and play the same way ever again. The transformation Mark and Denise have experienced has been cemented by the awakening they have shared. Their eyes have been opened too wide and the realities of their past issues and patterns have become far too clear to revert to the previous confines of their discontent.

The language of emotional debt has successfully helped many couples to lay bare their problems, take active steps towards resolution and inject an invigorating stimulus for communication, trust and love.

By utilizing the framework of debt resolution, partners can broaden the spectrum of loving exchange and achieve relationships of openness, respect, connection and caring. They will become debt-free, debt-wise . . . and truly EVEN.

Chapter 12

JHE FJNAL JNSJALLMENJ
A Parable

A pile of rocks is just a pile of rocks
until a single man contemplates it while holding
in his mind the vision of a cathedral.

- St. Exupery

The Emperor of an isolated kingdom conceived a great plan to build a wondrous highway which would link his empire to the far reaches of the world. In his wisdom, the Emperor understood that the time had come for his people to have the freedom to venture forth and experience the marvels and the perils of the outside world. On the day that the first stone of the highway was to be laid, the Emperor called his only son and daughter-in-law together to proclaim that he was appointing both of them as joint overseers of the monumental work.

"My beloved children, you have both shown yourselves to be sharp of mind and strong of will. I love each of you with all my heart and I have chosen to entrust to both of you the important task of supervising the construction of my great highway. I entreat you to share the responsibilities and to fulfill my dream of opening my kingdom to the farthest realms of the world. No duty to your father or your king has ever surpassed the importance of this endeavor."

Both were stunned by the Emperor's announcement, but they were each shaken for very different reasons. His own child, his son, who had always been devoted to his father and compliant to his every wish, spoke up first.

"Father, I am overwhelmed by your show of faith and confidence in me. You have always given me everything any son could ever want, and now you honor me further by your willingness to entrust such a great venture to me and my wife. But surely I am unworthy of overseeing the building of your great highway. I am already so much in your debt for your kindness and love that I dare not burden myself further by accepting such a noble appointment. So rather than granting me the royal responsibility of directing the construction, instead let me labor on your great highway by hauling stones and mortar so that my sweat and toil might one day repay you for all that you have bestowed upon me. Surely my wife should be the one to supervise such a wondrous undertaking."

The Emperor looked upon his son with loving eyes and spoke, "My Son, this debt which you feel you owe me is purely of your own making. I have always loved you and have expected nothing in return. But I hear the sincerity in your plea, and if you feel that you must bear stone and mortar to find peace within yourself, then do as you must."

The Emperor then turned to his daughter-in-law, the only child of his best friend, the deceased king of another region, and saw indignation and anger rising in her eyes. The girl, flushed with rage, spoke with a voiced filled with bitterness.

"Sire, I will not lower myself to the mundane task of overseeing the building of this meaningless road of yours. I am the first born of a royal line and such a position entitles me to the highest privilege and most noble esteem. Surely the lowly supervision of the movement of mere earth and rock is far beneath the dignity of a future queen. I will not tolerate such insult. I deserve far more and I will have it! Although I cannot return to my original kingdom, having chosen to marry your son and forsaking my heritage, I will this day leave your kingdom and venture forth to establish my true destiny as a revered queen in a new land. I can remain here no longer so long as my just due is withheld."

The Emperor looked sadly into the resentful face of his daughter-in-law and addressed her with compassion. "My daughter, my intent has never been to deny you or diminish you in any way. I have loved you with all of my heart as if you were born to me and I hoped to give you and my son everything you have ever wanted. But if you feel I owe you more and are determined to leave my kingdom to find your own peace, then do as you must."

Thereupon, both husband and wife left the Emporer's chamber—the daughter-in-law to hasten from the kingdom in search of her just reward, and the son to toil as a common laborer under the hot sun to build his father's great highway. The Emperor sadly watched the departure of his beloved son and daughter-in-law, knowing that both were imposing sentences of needless suffering upon themselves. Though the Emperor felt in his own heart that he had bestowed neither too little nor too much on either his son or his daughter-in-law, he was wise enough to realize that each one would have to find their own enlightenment. The Emperor's greatest hope was that both would resolve their own disquietude and would soon return to his kingdom, to each other, and to the Emporer's loving embrace.

Years passed. The daughter-in-law wandered throughout many foreign lands but failed to find another kingdom that would recognize her nobility or pay her proper homage. Her disillusionment grew as she was treated as a commoner in each new city she encountered. One day as her futile roaming led her to the outskirts of a dark forest, she was overtaken and beaten by robbers who bound her wrists with rope, blindfolded her and left her to die in the woods. With great effort she managed to rise to her feet and began to stumble ahead, blinded and lost. As she aimlessly wandered through the wilderness, her only wish was to return home and be reunited with her husband and father-in-law.

During these same years, the son had endured the pain and drudgery of hauling stones and mortar every day beneath the merciless sun. The Emperor's great highway now extended endless miles to the far reaches of the world. As he strained and labored with bloodied fingers and a weary back, the son came to feel that his duty to his father would soon be fulfilled and his debt repaid. He lived with the hope of one day returning to his wife's embrace and his father's palace, free from the lingering burdens that previously had thwarted his full acceptance of his father's love.

Finally, the day of the great highway's completion arrived. The honor of laying the final stone was bestowed upon the Emperor's son, since he had worked harder than any other laborer. As he stooped to position the last heavy stone and set it with mortar, a shadow fell across the smooth rock. He looked up and beheld a stranger, bound at the wrists, blindfolded and staggering near death. As the tortured stranger collapsed into his arms, the weary son removed the blindfold and was amazed to behold the face of his wife.

Revived by the embrace and freed from her bondage, his wife spoke with joy. "My husband, you have saved my life. But where am I now and how is it that you have found me? What road is this that has brought me to you?"

"My wife, this is the great highway that my father proclaimed. I have worked many years to build it, never knowing its final destination."

The wife gazed back across the wide expanse of carefully laid stones and cried out with gratitude, "I, who mocked your father's dream and belittled his grand vision, now at last see clearly. There was indeed a noble purpose to your father's master plan. This road, my husband, has surely been designed to be our pathway home. In his wisdom and forethought, my father-in-law has given me the most precious gift of all—my deliverance back into your and his loving care."

Her husband was overcome with his own joy and exclaimed, "I, too, have come to understand the true purpose of this highway. I, who had felt such a weight of debt to my father, have now been released from my burden through my arduous toil. Indeed, this road has been designed to be our pathway home—a pathway to each other and to him. Surely the Emporer knew that by laboring to build his highway, I would fulfill my sense of duty and be freed to return home and fully accept his loving care."

And so it came to be. Reunited, the husband and wife followed the highway back to the kingdom where they were joyfully welcomed back into the loving arms of the Emperor.

As generations came and generations passed, and as kingdoms rose and as kingdoms crumbled, the great highway withstood the touch of time. Sojourners from the ends of the earth—

the wealthy and the meager, the noble and the common—all traveled without fear along the pathway which led to wisdom and freedom. The highway extended without limit into the future—forever linking cities to cities, journeys to destinies, parents to children and husbands to wives.